PRAISE FOR
I WISH I'D QUIT SOONER

"Stuck under a toxic boss? You're not alone—and you're not powerless. Dr. Laura's essential guide offers practical strategies, expert insights, and real-world examples to help you navigate difficult workplace dynamics, protect your well-being, and take back control of your career."

—Mary Abbajay, author of *Managing Up: How to Move Up, Win at Work and Succeed with Any Type of Boss*

"A necessary punch of truth for a world that too often rewards the opposite."

—Paul McCarthy, speaker and author of *The F.I.R.E.D. Leader: Reinventing the Future of Leadership*

"Dr. Laura offers far more than an escape plan from toxic bosses: She delivers a blueprint for cultivating the kind of psychologically safe, high-engagement workplaces that reduce burnout and elevate performance. *I Wish I'd Quit Sooner* is equal parts wake-up call and roadmap—a rigorously researched, story-rich guide that transforms personal pain into the brighter future of a better workplace. If you care about people and results, this book belongs not just on your shelf but also as the cornerstone of your organizational culture."

—C. Allen Gorman, PhD, industrial-organizational psychologist and associate professor of management at the University of Alabama at Birmingham

"This book nails it. Clear structure, sharp insights, and zero fluff. Whether you're dealing with a toxic boss now or just want to understand what to avoid, it's a toolkit you'll come back to."

—Philip Vanhoutte, work well champion and coauthor of *The Smarter Working Manifesto*

"How I wish I had this book as a resource when I was working for a toxic boss! Dr. Laura's work is validating and provides a practical and emotionally supportive step-by-step plan to move from feeling helpless to regaining control of your career and life."

—Anonymous, VP in the Canadian energy industry

"Toxic bosses are incredibly painful, but do not define you nor your career. This book is a helpful guide to surviving a toxic boss and, more importantly, to recovering afterward and finding ways to thrive again."

—Andrew A. Schmidt, PhD, HR executive and creator of the Toxic Leadership Scale

I WISH I'D QUIT SOONER

Practical Strategies for Navigating and Escaping a Toxic Boss

DR. LAURA HAMBLEY LOVETT

SWP
SHE WRITES PRESS

Published in 2026 by
She Writes Press, an imprint of The Stable Book Group

32 Court Street, Suite 2109
Brooklyn, NY 11201
https://shewritespress.com
Library of Congress Control Number: 2025915289
Print ISBN: 979-8-89636-040-7
eISBN: 979-8-89636-041-4

Interior Designer: Tabitha Lahr

Printed in the United States of America

Names and identifying characteristics have been changed to protect the privacy of certain individuals.

I dedicate this book to all the resilient humans who participated in this impactful research. I admire their courage to leave a toxic boss, and their generosity to share their experiences to help others do the same.

CONTENTS

PART 3: Life Beyond a Toxic Boss

INTRODUCTION

Welcome to this journey into the world of toxic bosses. It is good to have you here. You may be reading this book because:

- Your ability to perform your job is being impacted by a toxic boss.
- A toxic boss is affecting your mental health and well-being.
- You're supporting someone who is working for a toxic boss.
- You have a heavy feeling in your heart when Monday morning comes along, knowing you have another week of dealing with your toxic boss.
- You feel trapped under your toxic boss, like there's no way out.

You do *not* need to feel this way. You have found this book for a reason. Come along on this journey with me to understand how you (inadvertently) ended up reporting to a toxic boss. Know that you're *not* alone, and that things *can* get better. A career and life post–toxic boss is within your reach—and this book will show you how to attain it.

How This Book Can Help You

This book is packed with tools and evidence-based advice for identifying, handling, escaping, and recovering from your toxic boss. Using the strategies in this book will save you energy, provide clarity, and help you navigate life beyond your situation. You will also learn from others who have gone through the toxic-boss journey; in this book I share countless stories from those who have lived under or escaped from their toxic bosses. These stories will help you understand the best path forward for your situation. Whether those featured in these pages finally *had enough* and quit or were let go—or, as I like to say, *set free*—their learnings serve as powerful tools to support *you* (or someone you care about) through this difficult part of your career journey.

This book will show you how to thrive in your work and life, even while dealing with a toxic boss. You'll learn how to assess your current situation, create a plan to survive and thrive, and gain the confidence to move forward in your career. You have the power to take back control of your career and life—it's all within your reach.

The Three Parts of This Book

PART 1: Suffering Under a Toxic Boss

This section dives into what working for a toxic boss looks and feels like. You will learn more about the 8 Toxic Boss Personas and what type you might be dealing with. Recognizing toxic boss behaviors and their impacts on your mental and physical health is the first step in your journey toward once again thriving in your career and life.

PART 2: Should I Stay or Should I Go?

This section explores your six main options and how having choices matters. You will learn about the power of creating a winning exit plan and how to shift your "psychological contract" and mindset to cope in the meantime. You will explore options such as filing a complaint, taking legal action, taking a medical leave, or quitting when "enough is enough." In addition, the potential of your boss deciding for you and letting you go before you can quit will be discussed.

PART 3: Life Beyond a Toxic Boss

The final section of this book focuses on your recovering and healing after working for a toxic boss. You will discover strategies and proven self-care methods from survivors who have gotten away and are now back in control of their lives and careers. You will feel empowered to proactively manage your career journey moving forward. You will get training on how to spot warning flags of toxic bosses so that you feel equipped to avoid another such boss. You will learn about how to trust a boss once again (because good ones are out there!). And finally, you will be inspired by stories of toxic boss survivors who are now thriving in their careers and lives.

My Journey into Researching Toxic Leadership

I've been compelled to research, write, and speak about toxic bosses, and their opposite, great leaders, by what I have seen and experienced in my twenty-five years in the field of industrial/organizational and career psychology. I've worked for consulting firms since 1999 and have run my own psychology practices since 2009, helping a wide range of clients with their leadership skills and career development.

I've also overseen a national team of career psychologists over the past sixteen years, and through that work have heard countless stories about the psychological impacts of toxic bosses across industries and levels in organizations. The thousands of individuals my team and I have helped have made clear that the number of toxic bosses in the workplace is ever-growing, and those bosses are wreaking psychological havoc on the workforce.

Before I started my own business, I had the misfortune of reporting to two separate toxic bosses, so I understand how stressful and difficult the experience can be to all aspects of your life. Each of these toxic bosses hurt me to the core, stole many nights of sleep, and made me think deeply about my career and path forward. The silver lining from these two experiences was that I have greater empathy for those going through their own toxic-boss journeys.

As a psychologist, I've had a front-row seat to the effects of toxic bosses seeping into every area of my clients' lives. Their situation affects not only their work motivation but also their families and, ultimately, their physical and mental health. If left unchecked, toxic bosses can impact the trajectory of people's careers and lives.

After seeing too many instances of toxic leadership at play while consulting for organizations, working with executives, and running employee engagement surveys, I asked myself—what could I do to help more widely?

I felt compelled to dive deep into this phenomenon so I could help as many people as possible navigate their toxic boss situations. I wanted to equip people to better spot the early warning signs, and to identify how toxic leadership plays out so they wouldn't have to feel they were alone or stuck.

As an adjunct professor of psychology, I supervise students on research projects and serve as a bridge between academic research and real-world issues impacting people and organizations. My current program of research on toxic leadership includes a qualitative study of employees across North America who have worked for and since left a toxic boss in the past five years that I conducted with Renee Pi in the winter of 2024. The toxic bosses we studied included managers through senior executives ranging from ages twenty to sixty-seven, with an average age of forty-three. This sample spanned many industries, including post-secondary education, energy, not-for-profit, agriculture, aviation, consulting, engineering, financial services, government, hospitality, legal, and healthcare. The average time a participant of the study reported to a toxic boss was twenty months—which is a long time to be subjected to this brutal type of reporting relationship.

In-depth interviews with each participant unveiled extensive themes and insights that have contributed to the content of this book. Recent follow-up surveys of hundreds of participants from North America have led to additional data that supports the explanations and recommendations you will find in these pages. For example, a survey completed in April 2025, with my research student Saichi Saini, of 212 North Americans found a strong and significant positive relationship between toxic leadership and burnout across four generations (boomers, generation X, millennials, generation Z). This further clarifies how harmful toxic leaders can be, leading to significant workplace stress and ultimately, in some cases, to employee burnout.

In addition, with my honors thesis student Lea Kalinovska, we completed another survey of 280 American and Canadian employees across industries in March 2025. This study expanded the definition of toxic leadership commonly used in the literature, and found that toxic leadership factors negatively impacted employee work engagement. These findings reinforce the expansive number of toxic behaviors these leaders demonstrate, and the harmful effects on employees' engagement with their work.

My hope is that the findings and strategies presented in this book will help as many people as possible navigate their toxic bosses and improve their lives.

Activities in Your Journal

This book includes activities that will help you reflect on the ways in which having a toxic boss has impacted you. I also recommend you keep a journal or notebook handy to capture the responses, thoughts, and feelings that emerge as you read. Journaling (noting your thoughts, experiences, and insights) will help you gain perspective and awareness that will better help you navigate and recover from a toxic boss. Be reflective and listen deeply to yourself, as much wisdom resides within you.

It's Never Too Soon to Start Documenting

A crucial recommendation from others who've escaped toxic bosses is for you to document their behaviors and incidents, ideally as they are happening. You can capture what has already occurred and any new incidents in your journal or in a separate document as you read along. A template and process for doing so will be described in Chapter 3.

Part 1: Suffering Under a Toxic Boss

"Toxic leadership is characterized by ongoing covert or overt behaviors that harm employees' engagement, productivity, and well-being. The impacts of toxic leadership include high employee turnover, low morale, increased stress, a fear-based culture, and decreased individual and organizational performance."

—Dr. Laura

PART 1 INTRODUCTION:

THE PLAGUE OF TOXIC BOSSES

Toxic bosses have been around as long as there have been bosses. They exist across every industry and country. They crawl into every level of leadership, from first-time supervisors through to senior executives. *Toxic leader* is what they are often called, but they don't deserve *leader* in their title. Instead, I prefer to refer to them as toxic bosses.

So, what is a *toxic boss* or *toxic leader*? The most used definition of *toxic leadership*—created by widely cited researcher Andrew Schmidt—is that they commonly demonstrate leadership patterns that are narcissistic, authoritarian, self-promoting, abusive, and unpredictable.[1] Further, their behaviors harm individuals in the organization, impacting both the individuals' and an organization's performance.[2]

Other researchers, including myself and my team, have investigated additional behaviors to expand the understanding of toxic leadership. Additional toxic boss behaviors can include dishonesty and manipulation, extreme control and excessive micromanagement, and unethical behavior, including corruption. Some toxic bosses are passive-aggressive, manipulating and working their toxicity in a more covert manner, while others are more openly abusive. There is no one specific type of toxic boss, and Chapter 2 in this book will help you identify which of the 8 Toxic Boss Personas best reflect your own toxic boss.

Toxic bosses are widespread. Anecdotally, most people I talk with can relate to having had one or having a loved one who has worked for one. Indeed, a 2023 survey found that 87 percent of professionals have had at least one toxic boss during their careers, with 30 percent encountering more than one.[3] Further research from a South African sample of 600 in the manufacturing industry found that 33 percent of leaders are capable of exhibiting toxic leadership.[4]

Regardless of how they express their toxicity—as covert or overt, politicians, or "bulls in a china shop"—one thing is for sure: These bosses greatly impact the human beings who report to them. Whether they learned their behavior from another toxic boss or they were always this way, they have the intent to hurt others and their actions are harmful. What they all have in common is a deeply negative impact on their employees, impeding performance, motivation, engagement, collaboration, and commitment. They can quickly destroy corporate cultures and lose great people, over time stunting company performance. Indeed, the top driver of employee attrition is bad bosses.[5]

Before we dig into your individual experience, it's key to distinguish *difficult bosses* from toxic bosses. A *difficult boss* is frustrating and not a good leader. They may be a poor communicator, a micromanager at times, and forget to show proper appreciation for your work. Many leaders are difficult to work for, but that doesn't make them toxic. People can learn how to navigate difficult bosses, and difficult bosses can learn skills and practice habits to improve their leadership competencies.

In other words, there is hope for every difficult boss that they'll eventually become a better boss.

In contrast, toxic bosses are extremely damaging and do *not* tend to improve or be open to improvement. You can survive working for a boss like this for a period of time, but you will never be able to thrive under a toxic boss. Here is a table to help you see the difference.

DIFFICULT BOSS	TOXIC BOSS
• Frustrating to work with, but not harmful to your mental/physical health	• Damaging to your mental/physical health
• Disorganized and prone to creating inefficiencies, but not to the extent that you are prevented from performing your work successfully	• Actively and intentionally impedes your job performance
• Poor communicator, but ultimately honest and means well	• Communication is dishonest and manipulative
• Absent-minded, inadvertently causing inefficiencies	• Deliberately withholds information
• Forgets to show appreciation at times, but gives you credit for the work you do	• Does not show appreciation and takes credit for your work

Note: Your boss does not need to demonstrate all the behaviors in each column to be a difficult or toxic boss. These are merely examples (though the more that apply in each column, the more likely your boss is either difficult or toxic, respectively). If your boss does not check any of the behaviors in the Toxic Boss column, you may still have a toxic boss, as these points are merely a sampling of the possibilities. You will learn more about the other ways toxic bosses operate as this book continues.

Toxic bosses take an enormous toll on people's mental and physical health, leading to serious health issues and burnout. One study discovered that workers reporting to toxic leaders were at greater risk for cardiovascular disease. Specifically, employees who reported to supervisors who created mistrustful environments were significantly more at risk for having four or more of the American Heart Association's Life's Simple 7 risk factors for cardiovascular disease.[6] Further, a study of Australian employees found that toxic workplaces increase the risk of depression by 300 percent.[7] According to the US Surgeon General, the workplace abuse from toxic bosses can lead to increased depression, heart disease, cancer, and other chronic illnesses.[8]

You don't want your health to be negatively impacted by a situation you have the ability to change; if it already has been harmed, however, please know that there is a healthier way forward in your career and life.

Trends in recent years, such as employees' increased expectations of better work–life balance, flexibility, and psychological safety, have challenged organizations to become more human-centric and supportive of people's mental health. I'm a big fan of remote and hybrid work options, but they do require people to juggle the competing demands of their work and lives, which can blur some boundaries. And remote work doesn't protect you from toxic leadership; this problem has continued to fester in the digital world, with abusive behaviors spanning from the boardroom to the Zoom room (I will delve into this more deeply later in the book).

This new post-pandemic era continues to evolve, with some companies continuing hybrid work arrangements and others mandating "butts in seats," with flexible work options evaporating. Cultures supporting inclusion, belonging, and mental health require human-centric leadership that cares about people beyond just being "resources." There is no place for toxic bosses in a human-centric culture, yet they continue to manipulate and abuse their way up corporate ladders, from enterprise organizations to start-ups, governments, and even nonprofits.

Toxic bosses may overtly harass and bully, or cause harm through a series of microaggressions. *Microaggressions* are defined as "verbal, behavioral, and environmental indignities that communicate hostile, derogatory, or negative racial slights and insults to the target person or group" (these could be related to someone's race, gender, sexuality, parental status, socioeconomic background, mental health, or any other aspect of their identity).[9] These behaviors must *stop*, and this book is a step toward educating and empowering people suffering under a toxic boss to strategically set themselves free.

CHAPTER 1:

SO, YOU'RE WORKING FOR A TOXIC BOSS? YOU'RE NOT ALONE!

"People don't leave bad jobs, they leave bad bosses."
—Anonymous

I will never forget the boss I briefly worked for in my first organizational consulting job in 2006 after completing my PhD in industrial/organizational psychology. I was eager to work hard and grow as a consultant, and open to doing whatever I could to help my boss and organization. Early on, an opportunity came up to create and deliver a presentation to a room full of corporate clients on employment branding. This topic was new to me, but I had the foundation of knowing how to gather the latest data and recommendations. Further, I was skilled at building slides, presenting, and facilitating by this point in my career. My answer to being asked to take on this opportunity was a resounding *yes*.

I worked hard to create an engaging session. My boss, who I later learned was referred to in our industry as the "Ice Queen," was on vacation while I was preparing, so I made sure to get feedback from two other senior consultants in the firm prior to delivering it to our corporate clients.

The day of my eagerly anticipated session, the Ice Queen was back in the office, and she attended. My body tensed as she stared at me, arms crossed, from the back of the training room. Her dark eyes pierced me with scrutiny; her thin lips formed not even the hint of a smile. Anxious energy filled me as I felt her gaze on me—I wanted nothing more than to shine. I spoke with passion to the busy room and facilitated the audience's questions to the best of my ability. When I was finished, I felt that I'd done a good job.

When the Ice Queen asked to give me feedback in the training room once the participants left, I was eager for her mentorship. My heart was pounding with the adrenaline of having just presented as I sat down across from her; I was nervous, but excited to learn from someone much more experienced than myself. Although I thought I'd done a good job, presenting clear points and recommendations and facilitating an engaging discussion, I knew I could improve and continue to grow as a presenter and facilitator, and I was eager to hear her thoughts.

The Ice Queen, in her crisp, steel gray business suit, sat me down with the two other consultants from our company who had attended—and launched straight away into the negative, scolding me for coming across as too "teacher-like," and for *embarrassing her* with actions she couldn't clearly articulate. She went on to say that my presentation was "simply not up to her standards," and made clear that she hadn't liked any part of it.

Her words were harsh and judgmental: *You did this wrong, this wasn't up to par, you didn't represent our brand professionally enough*. Her harsh litany of negative feedback turned my hands cold and clammy. I had to work hard to hold back my tears as I nodded politely, my shaking hand taking notes as best I could to capture her toxic barrage of "feedback."

Her icy "feedback" was not warmed by even a sliver of praise that day—but when I look back at that younger version of me, I know that although I certainly had room to grow, my performance did not warrant such toxicity. My presentation was clear and engaging, overall. The positive comments and thank-yous from participants at the end of the session showed me that they, our valued clients, had appreciated my efforts.

My shame was further amplified that day by the fact that the two other consultants, whom I will call Genevieve and Lucy, were watching. One was scribbling notes furiously and the other was avoiding eye contact with me, looking at the toxic boss as if she agreed. They were not given the chance to speak, nor did they try to jump to my defense.

As my eyes stung and I nervously twitched, my toxic boss finished chewing me out and went on to make small talk with the two consultants about their weekend plans.

I walked out of that room shaking.

Afterward, when I was alone in my office, Lucy, who had worked there longer, was particularly kind to me and affirmed that the Ice Queen frequently micromanaged. This was not the first time she had berated someone like this, she explained. In this case, she said, because the Ice Queen had been out of town while I'd been planning the presentation, she'd lost the opportunity to exert her usual level of control on this client presentation, and she'd made sure to punish me for that. Lucy emphasized that this was not so much about me but more about this particular boss, and that I should try not to take it personally.

My shoulders slumped. Easier said than done! Her behavior toward me exemplified how she'd earned her *Ice Queen* title.

This example may seem more or less extreme than what you've experienced, but it's helpful to note that toxic leadership takes on many different forms and impacts people in different ways.

Can you relate to getting negative feedback from a boss who was so harsh you had trouble processing it and felt your whole body reacting—pounding heart, trembling hands, clenched stomach?

In the days that followed the interaction with my boss, I lost sleep and grappled with whether to quit, asking myself whether this position was one where I could succeed and thrive. After weighing the facts and seeking advice from others who had worked for the Ice Queen, I knew it was not. Both logic and my intuition were screaming at me to leave the company as soon as I could. The conditions I was seeking for my growth and success—ones where I could take on challenging projects and grow through regular feedback in a supportive environment—did not exist in this workplace, and never would so long as this toxic boss was in charge.

I was not going to let the Ice Queen destroy my confidence. I gave my written notice, and left without getting a personal goodbye from my toxic boss. A tremendous sense of relief washed over me as I walked out those doors; I smiled ear to ear knowing that I'd never have to report to the Ice Queen again. The uncertainty of what I'd do next paled in comparison to being free. (Note: I don't take for granted that I was at a point in my life where I didn't have a family relying on me and had a supportive spouse who was employed. I know that's not always the case, and that as our financial responsibilities grow, often we need a job lined up before quitting. We will address these situations in this book.)

Within a few weeks I had found new work at a private psychology practice, a more supportive environment for my growth and development. I leaned on my circle of friends and family to support me and remind me that this Ice Queen experience had nothing to do with me, and my new job allowed me to continue growing my skills without a toxic boss lurking around me. Later, this early experience, layered in with other stories I encountered about toxic bosses in the years that followed, is what inspired me to embark upon researching, writing, speaking, and engaging in thought leadership on the topic of how to navigate toxic bosses with courage, confidence, and clarity.

Nearly two decades have passed since I was in that boardroom receiving the Ice Queen's feedback, but her toxic treatment of me at a vulnerable time in my early career still creeps into my mind on occasion. At times, I find myself dreading presentation feedback from my corporate clients because it triggers fears of not being good enough. All these years later, my heart sometimes races as I click open evaluations from my speaking or keynoting sessions. When these feelings emerge, I remind myself that the Ice Queen has melted far into my past.

In addition to the Ice Queen, I have experienced other toxic bosses in my career—and I want to thank them for helping me grow and evolve as a psychologist, organizational consultant, and leader. Having these lived experiences has attuned me to the impacts of these harmful behaviors on my clients, colleagues, friends, and people like *you*.

Most people have experienced at least one toxic boss, and most, like me, remember the behaviors and impacts this person had on them for the rest of their career and life. Remember, this is *not your fault*.

It's easy when you have the benefit of hindsight to think that you should have known better than to work with your toxic boss. Perhaps there were warning signs that you chose to ignore, or maybe you were thrust into the situation due to organizational changes; whatever the case, please know two things:

1. It is not your fault you ended up with a toxic boss.
2. You will take away important learnings and growth from this terrible experience.

The signs of a toxic boss are often subtle at first. Any of us can fall prey to a toxic boss, and we must not be hard on ourselves if we do. You made the decisions you did with the information that you had at the time, and you are continuing to evolve in your career and life. Instead of berating yourself for what's already done, spend your energy trying to understand where you are now so that you can *do* something about it.

The Emotional and Physical Pain Caused by Toxic Bosses

So, where are you at when it comes to the suffering you're enduring under your toxic boss? Let's explore the types of psychological and physical pain that toxic bosses commonly cause.

Just like there is no one type of toxic boss, how each person is impacted by toxic leadership varies widely. For example, your relationship may take a hit when you vent about work to your partner every evening or you don't have the energy for the fun activities you used to enjoy. Your physical health may be challenged by overeating and not exercising, as you feel too exhausted to work out and you overeat or drink to numb your pain. From your blood pressure and digestive health to your self-esteem and confidence, a toxic boss can ravage your overall well-being.

I would get angry at the way my toxic boss was treating me. Adrenaline would surge through me, which I knew was unhealthy. It felt like toxic waste in my body.

—MAGAZINE MANAGING EDITOR

I couldn't sleep or eat, I felt sick to my stomach working with this director. My heart sank with every episode (temper tantrum) he'd have on our set.

—HOLLYWOOD FILM PRODUCER

She really messed up my physical and mental health. It was so taxing. I was having eye twitches and back problems from the stress.

—HEAD OF PRODUCTION, PRINT AND COMMERCIAL INDUSTRY

Dr. Laura's Coaching Break: *How is your toxic boss affecting your well-being?*

Can you relate to any of the following?

- *Do you lie awake in the wee hours of Monday morning dreading your workday and week ahead?*
- *Do you look forward to your boss going on vacation, when you can (maybe) get a period of relief from their toxicity?*

- *When debriefing your workday with your partner, family member, or friend, do the actions of your boss that day take up most of those conversations?*
- *Do you and certain colleagues vent endlessly about the boss any chance you get?*

If you can relate to any of these statements, either in your current or past roles, you know full well how a toxic boss impacts your life. Each of the above experiences has come up frequently for participants in my research on toxic bosses. In addition, there are numerous other emotional and physical impacts that research participants have experienced that I want to introduce you to in the following exercise.

Place a checkmark beside all the following that you have experienced while working for your toxic boss (and are specifically a result of your toxic boss versus stemming from other workplace stressors), and write in your activity booklet or journal additional ways that each one has impacted you:

1. STRESS
   - ❑ I feel a high level of stress anticipating and interacting with my boss
   - ❑ My stress is constant, and difficult to get away from even when I'm not working
   - ❑ I am considering taking a medical leave as my stress has become too much
   - ❑ I am feeling mentally overwhelmed
   - ❑ I can't stop worrying about my situation with this toxic boss

Additional comments about my stress caused by my toxic boss (note these in your journal)

2. BURNOUT

- ❑ I am feeling exhausted and depleted of energy due to my toxic boss
- ❑ I feel removed or distant from my job, like it no longer matters
- ❑ I have negative or cynical thoughts about my work
- ❑ I feel like I can no longer do a good job under this toxic boss
- ❑ I no longer believe I have what it takes to contribute to my organization

Additional comments about my burnout caused by my toxic boss (note these in your journal)

3. ANXIETY

- ❑ I am constantly feeling anxious due to my toxic boss
- ❑ I am constantly worried when it comes to working for my boss
- ❑ I experience "Sunday night syndrome," where I dread having to work another week for my boss
- ❑ I fear interactions with my boss (e.g., meetings, phone calls, emails)
- ❑ I feel paranoid that my toxic boss is out to get me (e.g., that whatever I do may be watched, judged, or recorded; that my job and reputation are at risk)
- ❑ I have experienced panic attacks when it comes to working for my boss

Additional comments about my anxiety caused by my toxic boss (note these in your journal)

4. **DEPRESSION**

- ❑ I am suffering from depression*
- ❑ I am feeling very sad, unhappy, or low due to my toxic boss
- ❑ I have a negative voice in my head that says things will never get better at work
- ❑ I cry regularly about my situation at work
- ❑ I no longer enjoy or look forward to the things I used to

Additional comments about my depression/sadness caused by my toxic boss (note these in your journal)

*Note: There are free depression screening tools online, such as this one from Mental Health America: https://screening.mhanational.org/screening-tools/depression. If you have felt depressed for more than two weeks, it's imperative that you connect with your family doctor and a licensed therapist to more accurately assess your depressive symptoms and formulate a treatment plan.

5. **PHYSICAL SYMPTOMS**

- ❑ I am experiencing physical pain that I did not have before reporting to my toxic boss (e.g., muscle pain, stomach cramps, gut issues, headaches, jaw pain/clenching)
- ❑ My blood pressure is elevated
- ❑ I literally feel nauseous before meeting with my boss

Additional comments about my physical symptoms caused by my toxic boss (note these in your journal)

6. BEHAVIORAL CHANGES

- ❑ I am having difficulty either falling and/or staying asleep
- ❑ I have nightmares about working for my toxic boss
- ❑ My eating habits have changed since reporting to my toxic boss (e.g., eating more or less than before; eating more junk food)
- ❑ I am drinking more alcohol or using more drugs than before
- ❑ My self-care has suffered since working for my toxic boss (e.g., I'm not exercising or taking time for my wellness)
- ❑ I am binge-watching TV shows or other media to escape from my situation

Additional comments about my behavioral changes caused by my toxic boss (note these in your journal)

7. PERSONAL LIFE/RELATIONSHIP STRAIN

- ❑ My work situation is impacting my personal life
- ❑ My partner or family has been commenting that I am not myself (e.g., I'm short-fused or unhappy)
- ❑ My partner or family is expressing frustration that I am staying in my toxic job situation

Additional comments about my personal life/relationship strain caused by my toxic boss (note these in your journal)

8. OTHER IMPACTS

- ❑ I regularly feel angry that I'm in this situation
- ❑ My ability to focus and process information has been impacted due to my toxic boss (e.g., brain fog, having a hard time learning new things, blanking out)

- ❑ My memory has been impacted (e.g., vocabulary/ name recall, remembering important deadlines or the information I need to do my job properly)
- ❑ I feel stuck and trapped, like there is no way out from under my toxic boss

Additional comments and other impacts from your toxic boss not previously mentioned (note these in your journal)

Now take a deep breath. You may be feeling even more overwhelmed than before if you checked off a lot of these items. Hopefully, even if that is the case, this exercise has also validated for you just how much your toxic boss is impacting you. Know that these emotional and physical impacts are common for employees in your difficult situation, but you do *not* need to feel this way. Instead, there is light at the end of this toxic-boss tunnel; on the other side, positive feelings await you.

I have seen and heard firsthand how people feel once they learn to navigate, transition away from, and recover from a toxic boss. Once you're free, you'll once again feel:

- Positive about your work and career
- Confident about your skills and contributions in your position/field
- Empowered and in control of your career decisions
- Good about your coming workweek (i.e., you'll no longer dread Mondays)
- Motivated to do your best work

As I look back on that part of my life, I am able to recognize there were benefits to having gone through such a hard and stressful experience. These types of situations teach us a lot about ourselves, how not to take life for granted, and to always recognize your personal health and well-being are always more important than the chase for success and monetary gain.

—INVESTMENT COMPANY EXECUTIVE

I must admit that working in a toxic environment takes its toll on one's personal health and family. All of my family and I are so glad I am no longer working in a toxic culture where my VP continued to marginalize my integrity and self-worth. I always say when one leaves an organization they experience "freedom" not failure. Now I can say I feel healthier, mind, body, and spirit. I continually coach peers/ colleagues that if you feel psychologically unsafe and the environment is toxic, head for the exit before you become someone you do not wish to be. I learned a lot from a negative experience and now help others who are victims to grow and become strong.

—HEALTHCARE LEADER

When [my toxic boss] left, the whole structure changed. It was like the windows opened and that negative energy left. A siege and then a purge for many people.

—COLLEGE DIRECTOR AND FACULTY MEMBER

You now should have a better idea how working for a toxic boss impacts your well-being. Recognizing toxic boss behaviors and their impacts on *you* is the first step in your journey toward once again thriving in your career and life. In the next chapter, you will learn about the 8 Toxic Boss Personas and which type(s) of these you are dealing with.

Takeaways from Chapter 1

- ✓ If you have a toxic boss, you're not alone!
- ✓ Being in this situation is not your fault—it can happen to anyone.
- ✓ Toxic bosses cause emotional and physical pain.
- ✓ Toxic bosses can put strain on your personal life and relationships.
- ✓ You can navigate through and transition out of working for a toxic boss.
- ✓ There is light at the end of this toxic tunnel; on the other side, positive feelings await you.

CHAPTER 2:

WHAT TYPE OF TOXIC BOSS DO YOU HAVE?

"Toxic leaders are driven by ego, thrive on control, and suppress the creativity and innovation of their team."
—Brigette Hyacinth

There is not one specific style of toxic boss, but rather many different patterns of toxic behaviors. I have categorized these patterns or personas based on the hundreds of behaviors people who have suffered under toxic bosses have described to me in interviews for my research. This chapter will help you identify which personas best describe your toxic boss. Identifying your toxic boss will be helpful to further understand what you are dealing with and how to navigate your survival and transition.

Keep in mind that your toxic boss may demonstrate several of these eight different personas. There may be one persona that resonates most, or there may be many.

As you're reviewing each behavior, ask yourself if the behaviors sound like your toxic boss. Once you've reviewed these descriptions, you will later complete a checklist to determine which of these eight personas best describes your toxic boss.

The 8 Toxic Boss Personas

1. The Self-Serving Egomaniac

"Be patient," said Sam's boss, "your promotion will come if you keep producing top-notch reports and presentations."

Sam had heard this so many times over the past few years. He had busted his butt to make his boss shine to the CEO and board of directors, though he wanted to personally shine as well. His latest presentation, which he had spent several late nights finishing, was something he hoped to present to the board himself. He needed face time with the board so his talents could be recognized and he could secure his long-awaited promotion to the director level.

"I need to present this one, Sam, as this meeting has a lot of confidential information and only execs can attend," his boss explained when Sam asked to present his work.

The worst part was that Sam later opened the file and saw that his boss had removed Sam's name from the cover page of the presentation, clearly pitching it as his own work and taking full credit.

Sam felt utterly used and crushed. He reached out immediately to three recruitment firms.

The *Self-Serving Egomaniac* is all about themself. They are adept at getting others to do their work and then presenting it as their own. Equally as bad, they will not give you appreciation for your hard work and accomplishments along the way.

This type of toxic boss cares deeply about their own self-image and how others perceive them. Vanity is often at play, whether it's being in love with the sound of their own voice by dominating all conversations or being enamored with their self-image. For example, you may see them stopping to look at themself in the mirror regularly.

Self-Serving Egomaniacs will "suck up" to those higher up, always eager to climb to the top. They will *not* respect boundaries if they see an opportunity to advance their careers, often expecting you to work at all hours or be at their disposal and immediately respond to them no matter what else you are doing. They do not respect work–life balance, time zone differences, family and personal time, or cultural traditions and religious holidays. Their priorities must become your priorities.

These toxic bosses can be described as Machiavellian—meaning, they will use whatever means necessary to gain power. For example, if they are a vice president vying for a CEO position, they will happily climb over and sabotage their peers to get to the top. They will do whatever it takes to win, no matter the cost.

SELF-SERVING EGOMANIACS IN ACTION

[My boss] would not do anything on his own—every PowerPoint, memo, letter, and speech was produced by someone else. We all became adept at ghostwriting as him. Numerous articles were published in academic journals without the names of the real writers on them.

—LEADER IN HIGHER EDUCATION

2. The Control Freak

Natalie sat in her cubicle, letting her tears flow. She had just been dragged over the coals by her boss.

Natalie had successfully led a software implementation project that she was very proud of, and she knew the client was satisfied with her work. She now had an opportunity to build an additional implementation with this client that involved an AI tool from another department in her company. The client was excited about exploring this idea, and it had amazing revenue potential. This week, she'd sent an email to both her boss and the leader of the other department to explain her idea.

"Everything goes through me, Natalie," her boss scolded her, his face red and his brows furrowed. "I decide what other executives will be looped in once I vet any of your ideas." He didn't praise her former project's success nor appreciate her drive to bring up an additional software implementation opportunity.

She took a deep breath and wiped off her running mascara. When she logged onto her laptop she saw a positive email reply from the other department's leader about the idea, which she knew would make her boss even more furious, since he'd been copied on it. Her shoulders sagged. She wished she could report directly to this other leader.

The *Control Freak* needs to be in full control of everything, all the time. It's their way or the highway, and they do *not* want your opinions or ideas, even if they could lead to viable improvements or great progress. They are attached to their own vision, and although they may *say* they are open to feedback, their disinterest in and disregard for everyone else's input clearly says otherwise.

They especially do not like to be challenged. For example, if you have feedback that they have made an error or missed something of importance in a report or presentation, they will not appreciate hearing this. In fact, giving this feedback is likely to enrage them and lead them to punish you in various subtle or direct ways.

The *Control Freak* is hierarchical and acts as a gatekeeper, removing your access to others with higher authority. For instance, they will *not* want you to converse with their boss, or with anyone at or above their level. They will not hesitate to monitor and control your communications, as they are threatened by you making a positive impression on other decision-makers. For example, they will want to be copied on all emails or have you run information through them first. They will be hypervigilant about any threats to their reputation or position of power. This can make them come across as being highly secretive and paranoid.

A commanding and patronizing management style characterizes the *Control Freak*. They are overly critical of and quick to blame others, taking zero ownership for their own mistakes. When the *Control Freak* is in a more senior leadership role and they supervise managers, they are known to undermine the managers' leadership—for example, they will intervene to give direction or feedback to the team that is supposed to be the responsibility of the manager reporting to them. This will leave the manager feeling distrusted and disempowered.

CONTROL FREAKS IN ACTION

She had access to my manager's calendar and then ultimately asked for access to mine, and any time she met with me she asked, "Why are you meeting with this person? And what's the purpose of this meeting? And I notice all these gaps in your calendar and what's up with that?" This was an intense level of scrutiny and micromanagement.

—PROGRAM COORDINATOR IN HIGHER EDUCATION

3. The Dishonest Manipulator

Steve was shocked when he found out a colleague had been promoted to the vice president role in his company instead of him. His boss had acted like the role would be Steve's, and constantly complained about the recently promoted person's work.

"He's just not ready for that level," his boss had said about the other man just a few weeks earlier, "but if you keep going above and beyond on your account revenues, the role will be yours, Steve."

Watching maintenance put up a nameplate on his colleague's new corner office door, Steve felt sick to his stomach. He'd put in a ridiculous amount of overtime to prove himself to his boss over the past year, causing his marriage and health to suffer. Worst of all, he'd now learned that his boss had made the same promises to a third member of his team, who had confided in Steve that their boss had cut Steve down in front of her. Their boss was so utterly believable and charming, with her wide smiles and compliments, yet clearly was a wolf in sheep's clothing.

Steve began updating his resume.

This type of toxic boss is inherently dishonest. They create an environment of mistrust within their team and between colleagues. Lying or manipulating the truth is what they are good at. In fact, they lie so often that it becomes their entire way of operating, and they are good at making others think their lies are the truth.

The reasons this boss lies might be to get ahead, to achieve what they want, to protect people they are friends with, or to look good and "manage up" to their superiors, including senior executives or the company's board of directors. They can be excellent politicians.

Dishonest Manipulators do not appreciate being called out for their lies, and will manipulate their way into throwing you under the bus if you question them. They will not keep your confidence, so *do not* trust them with information you don't want shared widely. They will speak negatively about others behind their backs, and will not hesitate to do the same to you.

Dishonest Manipulators are sneaky and two-faced. They can put on the charm and act kind when they want or need something. They are not genuine nor authentic with their intentions or thoughts, often saying only what others want to hear. In other words, they will say one thing to you and the opposite to someone else—but in each case, they'll sound utterly believable. Or, their words won't match their actions; they will say one thing and do another.

Once the extent of their dishonest and manipulative behavior becomes clear, this type of boss will leave you feeling stunned and betrayed.

DISHONEST MANIPULATORS IN ACTION

I decided to move to a different city, which meant a transition to remote work. My supervisor was very supportive of the move and committed to changing my contract to reflect a remote office. She assured me that the move had been confirmed with HR and senior leadership and gave me the green light. She and I met weekly, and we discussed the move at each point, as this was a big transition for me. But a few days before the big move, she threw me for a loop. She shared, oh yeah, by the way, you're going to need to come back to the office, as it's not going to work anymore. I said, "What do you mean? You've given me the green light and I've sold my house. I don't have a place to live in the city. I can't just come back to the city." Her response was, "Change happens and you need to get better at navigating it."

—CONSULTANT

4. The Great Divider

Marsha sat down at the table for lunch with a friend and noticed her boss seated in a booth nearby with her two favorites. Marsha was left out, as always. They were laughing and carrying on like close friends would. The hardest part was that those favored colleagues got given the new and exciting work, while the crap stuff was left for Marsha.

She recalled her last one-on-one with her boss, where she'd asked if she could attend the conference in Denver that she knew the favorites were approved for. "No, Marsha, we have a limited budget and we need you here to take care of things while we're away," her boss had explained in her condescending voice. "We can revisit this next year."

Marsha wished she could quit on the spot, but she would be walking away from the remaining pension she would need in order to retire in seven years. She felt stuck and disheartened.

The *Great Divider* thrives at causing dissension among the team. They are skilled at pitting people against each other and creating a psychologically unsafe environment with an undercurrent of fear. If you are a manager, they may try to pit you against your direct reports by undermining your leadership. They will divide you from your peers, creating silos and toxic competition. They are adept at triangulating relationships, creating significant mistrust among colleagues. By causing these damaging divides, the *Great Divider* ensures that their people will not unite and rise against them (if you think this sounds suspiciously like a dictator, you are correct!).

The *Great Divider* likes to choose favorites, thereby creating an in-group and out-group. Their favorites are often people who are similar to them or are their friends. They will commonly promote or compensate people based on whom they like and who is a yes-person who doesn't challenge them, while removing supports, opportunities, or perks for those who are in the out-group. They are known to shut out and marginalize those whom they want to be out. Rest assured that if you question or challenge a *Great Divider*, you will be punished or excluded, potentially to an extent that will negatively impact your career development and growth, and possibly even put your job in peril.

GREAT DIVIDERS IN ACTION

I was invited to the first in-person event we'd organized since I'd joined the unit during COVID. The event was a lunch near campus, at the invitation of a group of Latin American consuls, ambassadors, etc. There were between fifteen and twenty participants at the luncheon and my presence had already been confirmed and listed on the agenda. The Friday before the event, in our weekly meeting, my boss informed me that I would not be attending the luncheon because there was no room for me at the table. Instead, the university's attendees would be the president, himself, and my direct report. I challenged him on this, citing a break of protocol and the optics of sending three men and skipping the woman when a good number of the consuls and ambassadors were women. He responded that he would think about it, but during our following weekly meeting, he reiterated his decision and stated that I was to refrain from attending.

—UNIVERSITY DIRECTOR OF
INTERNATIONAL EDUCATION

> *The executive team of the hotel I worked in middle management for pitted all the departments against one another. We, the middle managers, had good working relationships and were very open with communication. The executives didn't like this and said we could not communicate with each other anymore, saying it was creating workplace gossip. They had us sign forms that we wouldn't communicate. I became quiet and internalized. This workplace was toxic and I knew I couldn't stay.*
>
> —FOOD AND BEVERAGE OPERATIONS MANAGER

5. The Unethical Corruptor

"I think we should include all the results, as we promised everyone in the department would get back a report of the aggregate results," explained Chen in a one-on-one MS Teams video meeting with his boss.

"Chen, there is way too much detail, and I don't want the department having to spend hours reading this. My job is to get the highlights to them that matter. You always get buried in too much detail," she lectured, crossing her arms and shaking her head. "Detail is the enemy of efficiency."

Chen was disgusted that his boss had cut out most of the negative feedback that had been collected about her own leadership—comments such as her being abrasive, unfair, not listening, playing favorites, and not caring about the team—and he felt sick to his stomach about how wrong it was to alter survey results. This employee survey had been conducted by HR, as turnover was high on the team. But his boss had bullied HR into allowing her access to the full data so she could present it to her department. Chen had suggested an external firm be used, but of course his boss had denied that option, as that would have prevented her from controlling the results.

"Chen, I trust you," she said. "I hired you because you're smart and trustworthy and so long as you're trustworthy, you will get great bonuses like last year. You are not to share this full report anywhere. Yes, there is some stuff I can learn from in there, and I will, but what's important is that the department has never been stronger financially and we will continue being the best at what we do. The rest is noise."

Chen nodded, although his ethical compass was screaming at him. He knew he needed to find another role before his own reputation was damaged by being associated with this unethical woman.

The *Unethical Corruptor* is a toxic boss who lacks integrity to the point of corruption. Their decisions and actions are unethical, whether that means misrepresenting a product, reporting information inaccurately, lacking financial integrity, tampering with survey results, or manipulating compensation. Their corrupt acts will often serve their own career progression or pocketbook. Whatever they are stealing from the organization, be it time, money, information, or other resources, they will expect their employees to cover for them, thereby risking their own integrity.

The *Unethical Corrupter* may also practice discriminatory hiring practices, such as asking illegal questions (e.g., about whether the candidate plans to start a family) or not hiring people for illegal reasons. They feel they are above the law, and will minimize or deny these behaviors altogether. If they are trying to get rid of you, they will likely ignore the rules of employment law, cutting corners and abusing your rights, including pushing you to sign an NDA when laying you off without allowing you enough time to review it with your lawyer.

UNETHICAL CORRUPTERS IN ACTION

She fired the IT director and hired a new one, a young one with not a lot of experience whom she could manipulate and control. As she wanted to know who gave her negative feedback on an employee survey, she had him give her access to the system to find out who submitted previously stated anonymous questions.

—FORMER VICE-CHAIR, PRIVATE SCHOOL'S BOARD OF DIRECTORS

6. The Abusive A-Hole

Pak fisted his hands while his heart raced. His boss, a supreme jerk, had just made a derogatory remark about "gays" at a team meeting. Pak was gay and was open about this with the team, and couldn't believe his ears.

The boss then turned to the one woman in the meeting, Leslie. "Hey, Leslie, can you take the minutes again? Women do that best," he said.

Leslie was speechless; she bowed her head and was clearly offended yet again.

Not only do we have a homophobic boss, but a sexist one as well, Pak thought angrily.

Their boss's bullying behavior had gotten progressively worse over time, and Pak knew they had to go to HR, but worried about being fired if he was found out.

The *Abusive A-Hole* persona is what we often think of when it comes to toxic bosses. It encompasses the abuse, bullying, and harassment that these horrible humans are capable of. The behaviors of *Abusive A-Holes* include threatening your job (e.g., making you feel replaceable, issuing ultimatums), derogatory and disrespectful comments, and personal attacks. They may insult your competence or intelligence, diminish your abilities, and be condescending about your work. Those who are verbally aggressive will yell, swear, and fly into rages. Just like the cycle of abuse in romantic relationships, abusive supervisors may show remorse after being aggressively abusive, only to repeat the cycle again. For example, one of my research participants would get a bouquet of flowers after each abusive encounter with her toxic boss.

Harassment is common for *Abusive A-Holes*, including specific instances of racism, sexism, sexual harassment, or derogatory remarks toward minority groups. Bullying behavior is common among *Abusive A-Holes*, and it's as if they thrive on hurting or breaking people. They also tend to tolerate this type of abusive and bullying behavior from others in the workplace or customers, not having your back when you need them to.

ABUSIVE A-HOLES IN ACTION

I had hip surgery during the pandemic. I delegated my work to someone but [my boss] was not a huge fan of him. Five days after my surgery, she calls me at home: "It's just your hip, your head is fine. You need to get back to work, this is really bad for your career."

—VICE PRESIDENT OF AN ENERGY COMPANY

My boss shamed me regularly, making me feel like I wasn't holding things together. It got to the point where I would dread sending her emails, as I knew her replies would belittle me (for example, she would curtly reply with "as mentioned" or "per the below conversation" and proceed to make me feel stupid). Nobody else made me feel this way and I was thriving everywhere except with her.

—EDITOR

> *My boss left carnage in his wake. A lot of the people at the bank left and were never the same again. I mean, there were times I would feel like throwing up on my way to his office because I didn't know how he was going to react.*
>
> —ADVISOR TO SENIOR VP,
> FINANCIAL SERVICES/INVESTMENTS

7. Disordered Personalities: The Narcissist and Sociopath

"Yep, another 100 layoffs under my belt, that would make it about 2,000 over my career," bragged Tanya.

Kent couldn't believe what he was hearing as he sat in her big corner office overlooking the city.

"Don't be so sensitive about it, Kent—they are just resources," Tanya said. "After all, we are in human RESOURCES, and they come and go like deposits in the bank."

"I just think of their families," Kent replied, his stomach churning with disgust at his boss's utter lack of empathy. "It's a tough market and they may not land other jobs quickly this year."

"Kent, Kent, Kent. Not our problem! Stop being a bleeding heart. Maybe you should've gone into social work. What happens to them after they walk out of here is not our problem. If they decide to jump off a bridge, that's because their overall life is a mess, and definitely not our problem."

Kent's heart pounded and his disdain for Tanya increased even more. He knew he had to leave but felt trapped, given the sorry state of the labor market. He hated every meeting with her and needed to get out as soon as he could.

> *He wasn't a clinician, but the team had used the words "narcissist" and "sociopath" to describe Tanya, and he felt they weren't wrong.*

Narcissism is a term that has become part of our everyday lingo—but narcissistic personality disorder is a formal clinical diagnosis involving a "pervasive pattern of grandiosity (in fantasy or behavior), need for admiration, and lack of empathy."[1] People use (and sometimes overuse) the term narcissist widely to describe people they know personally—at work, in the media, and in politics—who are highly self-absorbed, lack empathy or appreciation for how they impact others, seek out approval and status, display arrogance and entitlement, and can be incredibly charming. Narcissism is on a continuum, and it's at the extreme of this continuum where the most damage is done. When it comes to toxic bosses, it's the *extreme* narcissist that stands out as a truly damaging boss.

The *Narcissist* boss has a grandiose sense of self, combined with zero empathy. These bosses can be very charismatic, beguiling, and smooth, yet do immense damage to the self-confidence and psyches of their direct reports. Due to many clients struggling with this type of toxic boss, I decided to do a series of four episodes on my podcast *Where Work Meets Life*™ in 2022, for which I was joined by two widely renowned experts and best-selling authors on narcissism. These episodes have been some of the most popular in my podcast's history, underscoring just how many people are struggling with *Narcissist* bosses at work. (See the Resources section at the end of this book for these specific episodes.)

Even more disturbing are *Sociopath* bosses, who take pleasure in the pain of their direct reports. In the *DSM-5*, sociopathy is categorized as an antisocial personality disorder, and involves the presence of a pervasive pattern of disregard for and violation of the rights of others.[1] These behaviors tend to begin by age fifteen and to present themselves in various contexts.

Sociopaths are often very intelligent, and they use their intelligence to intentionally manipulate and hurt people. Alongside their disregard for the rights of others, they have no capacity to feel guilt, remorse, or empathy.

DISORDERED PERSONALITIES IN ACTION

I had initially not cried because I don't tend to, and I could feel that she wanted me to cry. She just kept on going until I did cry. And then, as soon as I did start crying, her whole demeanor changed. She asked me if she could hug me. It was just so disconcerting. She just was super, super cold—and then as soon as I broke down, it was like she wanted to comfort me, which was really horrible.

—FORMER DIRECTOR OF A NONPROFIT ORGANIZATION

He wasn't knowledgeable about his job, yet when anyone questioned him he became defensive, abrasive, and condescending. He had an attitude of entitlement, believing that whatever he said was true and nobody could disagree with him.

—FILM PRODUCER

He'd pop by my desk and eat up forty minutes talking about himself. One day I told him I had one minute to talk because I was busy. He gave me a "look" and I knew he'd punish me later on. After that, it was easier to just listen to his ramblings than deny them.

—SENIOR COMMUNICATIONS ADVISOR

8. The Gaslighter

Gabrielle was shaking as she approached her boss. She had barely slept the night before, which was an all-too-common occurrence these days. Since beginning to report to Ron earlier that year, she'd started to feel like a shell of the woman she'd once been.

She approached his door and he ushered her in.

"Gabrielle, sit down. I'm not gonna beat around the bush. You dropped the ball on my filing that was due end of day yesterday." He shook his head and crossed his arms sternly.

"I'm sorry, but you told me the Redburn case was the priority and that one could wait until the weekend," Gabrielle nervously explained. She remembered this conversation, right at this desk, a week ago.

"That is simply not true, Gabrielle." He furrowed his brow. "I notice you are forgetting a lot of what I tell you. How can I trust you as my right hand if you don't listen to what I need?"

Gabrielle didn't know what to say. Maybe the lack of sleep was jumbling her memory. Yet she knew the truth—she had never messed up this sort of thing in her whole ten years as a paralegal, and she hadn't messed it up this time.

"I need you to get your head on properly, Gabrielle, so I can trust you," he ordered. "Now go do that filing as fast as you can and let me know immediately when it's finished."

"Yes, sir," Gabrielle said, quickly leaving. She felt like she was losing her mind, and was likely to lose her job. She wished she had the energy to start applying elsewhere, but who would want her in this state?

A toxic boss who is a *Gaslighter* is skilled at playing mind games to make you feel incompetent at best, and mentally unstable at worst. The American Psychological Association defines gaslighting as "Manipulating another person into doubting their own perceptions, experiences or understanding of events," and this is what a *Gaslighter* boss does. They will deny or change their accounts of past events, conversations, or commitments you know happened and clearly remember. They are so convincing that you begin to doubt whether these happened. Further, their instructions are often contradictory and confusing, leaving you to further doubt that you can meet their expectations. Put simply, a *Gaslighter* can make you believe you are losing your mind.

Working under a *Gaslighter* will undermine your confidence, as they will regularly criticize your capabilities and decisions, leading you to doubt yourself and fear retribution. *Gaslighters* will increasingly shame you privately as well as humiliate you publicly.

Gaslighting is a serious type of emotional abuse that can have long-term impacts on your self-confidence and mental health. The experience of being gaslit is extremely difficult, and you will likely require a longer recovery period to regain your sense of confidence and self-esteem after working with this type of boss.

GASLIGHTERS IN ACTION

He would tell me to do things a certain way (or to write things a certain way), and then when the senior approver didn't like it, he'd come back to me and say he'd never told me to do that. Lots of that happened. Outright lying when things didn't work out in his favor, despite having followed his direction.

—SENIOR COMMUNICATIONS ADVISOR

Dr. Laura's Coaching Break: *What personas best describe your toxic boss?*

Below is a behavioral checklist organized by each of the eight toxic boss personas. Check off all those that describe your toxic boss. The more behaviors that apply from any given persona, the more likely it is that you are dealing with that type of toxic boss. You will see if one or more personas are the most indicative of your boss. Knowing what you're dealing with will help you better navigate their behaviors as you make your plan to transition.

TOXIC BOSS PERSONA	BEHAVIORS
1. The Self-Serving Egomaniac	❑ Takes credit for your work ❑ Does not show appreciation for your work or accomplishments ❑ Completely self-absorbed ❑ Deeply cares about how others perceive them ❑ Good at sucking up to higher-ups ❑ Has demonstrated a willingness to use whatever means necessary to gain power ❑ Does not respect your work–life boundaries; expects you to be available whenever needed TOTAL: ________ /7

TOXIC BOSS PERSONA	BEHAVIORS
2. The Control Freak	❑ Micromanages ❑ Does not want your opinions or ideas ❑ Reacts very negatively to being challenged ❑ Acts as a gatekeeper, preventing your access to those at higher levels ❑ Monitors/controls your communications ❑ Highly secretive and paranoid ❑ Commanding and patronizing TOTAL: ________ /7
3. The Dishonest Manipulator	❑ Frequently tells lies ❑ Words don't match actions—says one thing, does another ❑ Charming and nice when they need something ❑ Creates an environment of mistrust between their team/with colleagues ❑ Good at manipulating situations so they don't take any blame or ownership ❑ Does not keep confidences ❑ Speaks negatively about others behind their backs TOTAL: ________ /7

TOXIC BOSS PERSONA	BEHAVIORS
4. The Great Divider	❑ Pits team members against each other ❑ Creates a psychologically unsafe environment ❑ Triangulates relationships ❑ Plays favorites (e.g., hiring or promoting people they like) ❑ Shuts you out or marginalizes you ❑ Creates toxic competition among team members or colleagues ❑ Undermines your leadership by pitting your direct reports against you TOTAL: ________ /7
5. The Unethical Corrupter	❑ Severe lack of integrity ❑ Makes unethical decisions ❑ Steals from the organization (e.g., time, money, or other resources) ❑ Expects you to cover up their corrupt actions and decisions ❑ Practices discriminatory hiring practices (e.g., asking illegal questions, not hiring someone for illegal reasons) ❑ Acts as if they are above the law ❑ Manipulates data to make them look better (e.g., financial data, survey results, other reporting) TOTAL: ________ /7 ⇨

TOXIC BOSS PERSONA	BEHAVIORS
6. The Abusive A-Hole	❑ Threatens your job and compensation ❑ Makes derogatory and disrespectful comments ❑ Bullies you ❑ Makes personal attacks (e.g., against your competence, intelligence) ❑ Flies into rages (e.g., yells, swears) ❑ Makes racist, sexist, and/or homophobic remarks ❑ Tolerates abusive behavior by others (e.g., colleagues, customers) TOTAL: _________ /7
7. The Narcissist or Sociopath	❑ Grandiose sense of self ❑ Lacks empathy ❑ Seeks approval and status ❑ Arrogant and entitled ❑ Can be incredibly charming ❑ Very intelligent, but uses this to manipulate and hurt others ❑ Lacks guilt or remorse TOTAL: _________ /7

TOXIC BOSS PERSONA	BEHAVIORS
8. The Gaslighter	❑ Plays mind games ❑ Makes you feel incompetent ❑ Makes you feel mentally unstable ❑ Denies events, conversations, or commitments that you clearly remember ❑ Blames you for problems and mistakes that aren't your fault ❑ Gives you contradictory instructions or feedback ❑ Humiliates you in front of others TOTAL: ________ /7

Now that you've finished this checklist, you should have a better sense of which kind of toxic boss you're dealing with. The higher the score in each subsection, the more your toxic boss fits that persona. If you have checked off at least four of the behaviors in one of the personas, it's pretty clear your toxic boss is demonstrating the behaviors of that persona. It's not about the overall scores, though, but rather about the types of toxic behaviors that are damaging your well-being and productivity.

Know that this list is not exhaustive, as there are many more harmful behaviors a toxic boss can engage in, and each situation is unique. It's key to note those behaviors as they occur, as our memories can be selective when dealing with stressful or trauma-inducing events. Capturing as much description as you can while the incident is still fresh in your mind will be important as you make decisions about your path forward.

If your boss does not resemble any of these personas, it may be that you're dealing with a difficult but not *toxic* boss. The difference between a difficult and a toxic boss is that a difficult boss can be managed and does not significantly impact your overall well-being and performance, as is the case with a toxic boss. You can learn to manage and work for a difficult boss if you feel the benefits outweigh the frustrations. (Books like Mary Abbajay's *Managing Up* provide great advice for working with and thriving under difficult bosses; check out where to find the podcast episode I recorded with Mary in the Resources section at the end of this book.) But when it comes to a toxic boss, leaving your position is ultimately your best—and, if you want to preserve your mental well-being, likely your only—option.

You now should have a better sense about the personas and associated behaviors of toxic bosses, and which category your toxic boss falls into. Hopefully you have a clearer sense and ways to describe what you are dealing with. In the next chapter you will learn about the options that lay ahead for you in deciding if you should stay or go.

Takeaways from Chapter 2

- ✓ There are eight main personas of a toxic boss, although this list and the behaviors are not exhaustive.
- ✓ Your boss may fit one or more of these personas.
- ✓ All of these personas are toxic and damaging to your mental health, physical health, and work success.

✓ You are not alone; millions of others have also suffered under toxic bosses, as you can see from the stories and quotes shared in this chapter.

Part 2: Should I Stay or Should I Go?

"A bad boss is like a disease of the soul."
—Chetan Bhagat

PART 2 INTRODUCTION:

WEIGHING YOUR OPTIONS

In Part 1 of this book, you learned about toxic bosses, including their various personas. You also learned about the psychological and physical impacts of a toxic boss. Clearly, a toxic boss is not good for your health and well-being.

Working under a toxic boss will also impact other aspects of your work and feelings about your job. We will explore these impacts in this section as you determine the costs/benefits of staying or leaving your job.

Exploring your options and knowing that you have choices will be discussed in Chapter 3. You have more choices than you might think when it comes to staying at or leaving your job. You will learn about the power of setting a "good riddance" (GR) date, and how to shift your *psychological contract* and mindset to cope in the meantime, and we'll also discuss options like taking a medical leave. In Chapter 4, we'll discuss the choice of quitting when *enough is enough* or when your boss decides for you and lets you go.

So, settle in and continue on this journey with me so you can make a plan that's best for *you*.

CHAPTER 3:

CHOICE MATTERS—CONSIDERING YOUR OPTIONS

"The most dangerous place to stay is under the rule of a toxic boss—it erodes your self-worth, distorts your reality, and trains you to tolerate dysfunction. Leaving isn't quitting—it's reclaiming your dignity."

—Dr. Ramani Durvasula

Tessa daydreamed about telling her boss to F off and storming out of the building. She cursed in her mind during meetings as he talked over her and made her head hang low with feelings of not being good enough.

If only she could just quit—but she had a mortgage and other debts. She had worked so hard to get to the Team Lead level and was finally earning a good salary and benefits, and the job market out there wasn't great.

When she thought about taking a lower-paying job, her heart raced with anxiety. She feared having to take a huge salary cut—or, even worse, not finding a job at all. She felt stuck and wondered how she could possibly ever get out from under this a-hole.

It's common to feel trapped under a toxic boss. The stability and security of your salary and benefits hold enormous weight. People describe being financially trapped longer term, whether that means being tied to stock options, a pension, or other long-term incentives, as wearing *golden handcuffs*. Employees may also fear that their toxic boss will find out if they apply to other jobs, or feel anxious that they won't get hired anywhere else. Plus, victims of a toxic boss may be terrified to whistle-blow by revealing information about their boss to someone in a position of authority or a neutral third party. They fear retribution if their toxic boss finds out, so they end up staying, hoping things will improve or that the company will reprimand or fire the toxic boss.

Unfortunately, improvement rarely happens. The behaviors of toxic bosses tend to get worse over time, and their victims continue to suffer. Their employees' well-being continues to erode, and their employees' work can be impacted as well. Staying at a job with a toxic boss can lead to a self-fulfilling prophecy that goes something like this:

1. Your toxic boss erodes your confidence and well-being. For example, you feel not good enough at your job.
2. You feel disengaged at work. You lose the motivation and energy to put in the effort you used to.
3. Your quality of work and productivity suffer. For example, your attention to detail, focus, memory, efficiency, and problem-solving abilities deteriorate.

- Your toxic boss notices that your work is no longer up to standard (e.g., you're making mistakes and/or missing deadlines) and now has ammunition to performance-manage and fire you should they so choose.

This self-fulfilling prophecy doesn't have to become a reality for you. One thing that most people I have spoken with about toxic bosses say is that they wish they had left sooner—that staying negatively impacted their health and productivity. Their advice to others was, "Get out as soon as you reasonably can." Not a single person I've come across has expressed regret about leaving a toxic boss, but *many* have said they regret staying as long as they did. Indeed, an international survey of 1,000 employees about career regrets revealed that 58 percent of respondents regretted staying at a job too long.

Document, Document, Document

As you determine the choices ahead, if you haven't done so already, I recommend that you begin documenting your toxic boss's behaviors and any incidents that occur. Think about the past, and capture anything new. This can be written, typed, or even recorded on your phone (in most states and provinces it's legal to do this last one, but worth it to check in your jurisdiction first). This is important for two reasons:

1. You will have descriptions, dates, and evidence should you choose to file a complaint or take legal

action in the future (it's so easy to forget exactly what happened after the fact, especially because your situation may be highly emotional). *Note: We will be exploring the options available to you shortly.*
2. The act of documenting will help you recognize just how much you are going through. This could both help you realize sooner just how toxic your boss is, and aid you in your healing as you process what you've endured and recovered from.

To document, you can use an Excel file or table that you save on your personal computer, or you could even write it in a notebook. Do *not* save this on your work computer or phone, only on your personal devices. Why? Because you do not want this file to be stored on any company platform in case it could be accessed by your boss (yes, although rare, that can happen if your toxic boss is particularly paranoid and driven to uncover what you might be communicating about them). Further, you want to ensure you will always have access to this information, and in the event you are suddenly let go and cut off from your files, you will lose that access if it is stored on a work device. Any proof that comes from work, such as toxic emails or messages, should be forwarded or screenshotted so you have personal records of these.

Here is an example of how you might record what happens over time:

DATE/ TIME	BEHAVIOR OR INCIDENT	IMPACTS	PROOF
July 13, 2024	*My boss berated me in a team meeting and on a follow-up Teams message for not delivering something I was never told to do.*	*I felt humiliated and very stressed. Sick to my stomach. Had trouble focusing on a report I had to write that afternoon.*	*Screenshot of Teams message. My colleague Sandy was in the meeting and witnessed this. She has had similar experiences to me.*
July 28, 2024	*Boss gave one of my newer colleagues the lead role on a project that I successfully delivered last time, even though she promised this role to me four months ago.*	*I felt lied to. This felt very unfair. Seemed like favoritism, as new colleague has no experience with that type of project.*	*Email from four months ago congratulating me on job well done on project and saying that I could lead the next one.*

This should be a working document that you go back to iteratively as you remember things to add. Situations and behaviors that seemed innocent at the time may stand out as they become repeated behaviors or patterns. You don't necessarily need to organize this chronologically; you can always sort it later. According to many others who have been through the experience of working for a toxic boss, this is a powerful exercise and antidote against gaslighting. (As a reminder from

Chapter 2, the *Gaslighter* is skilled at playing mind games to make you feel incompetent or mentally unstable. They will deny or change their accounts of past events, conversations, or commitments you know happened and clearly remember, which is why having clear documentation will be incredibly helpful.)

How Is Your Toxic Boss Impacting Your Work?

As you're navigating your choices, be honest with yourself about how your toxic boss is impacting your work. The impacts on your well-being that we already discussed are critically important. Add to these your ability to do your job effectively, which is not only essential for your annual performance but also for your longer-term career trajectory.

Remember that we all have different perceptions, based on our own experiences and how we are wired, of what leadership should look like. The challenges you experience with a toxic boss may not present themselves to a different colleague who is able to work with them. The boss may treat that colleague differently than they treat you, and consequently their dynamic is more sustainable. It's your own perception and experience that matters.

In so many cases, a toxic boss can derail the work of someone who has previously been a great employee. It's unfortunate when someone who was a strong performer now lacks the confidence and energy they once had, and their fear of making mistakes has become a reality.

TOXIC BOSS WORK IMPACTS IN ACTION

You deserve to work for employers who value your time and passion. I feel like if you're belittled consistently in your position, it's not only really demeaning to your work abilities, but also to your confidence and your judgment of yourself. And I feel like it's not worth it . . .

—LEGAL ASSISTANT

In the film world, you're only as good as your top person. When the director is having a temper tantrum, it demoralizes the mood on set and everyone's enthusiasm for the project. His toxic behaviors brought down people's performance . . . and they began not to care about the project.

—HOLLYWOOD FILM PRODUCER

Dr. Laura's Coaching Break: *How is your toxic boss affecting your work effectiveness?*

Now it's time to reflect on your situation. Below are mini-checklists based on each area of common impacts that a toxic boss can have on your work (including your feelings about work and your effectiveness in the job). The impacts that follow come from survivors of toxic bosses in my research. The more of these you check off in each section, the more likely it is that your current boss is actively impairing your ability to do your job effectively.

When you're done, you will add up these scores to determine if you are in a Red Alarm, High Risk, or Moderate Risk Zone, and determine the risks to your work effectiveness in each zone. Once you've established all this, we'll talk about what to consider doing about it.

TOXIC BOSS WORK IMPACT #1: CONFIDENCE AND SELF-ESTEEM
❑ I find myself doubting myself/my abilities at work
❑ I'm increasingly feeling incompetent
❑ I'm losing my voice or ability to stand up for myself
❑ I'm feeling insecure in my job
❑ I'm blaming myself for being in this situation
TOTAL: ________ /5

WHAT YOUR SCORE MEANS:

The higher your score in this section, the more your work confidence and self-esteem are being impacted by your toxic boss. If you didn't check any of these items, it's good to know that your self-confidence hasn't yet been impacted by your situation. Stay aware of these potential impacts and watch out for these feelings as warning signs, but for now, feel free to skip to the next checklist. If you did check some of these items, pay close attention to the areas you've answered yes to, as well as on each chart that follows in this section.

Warning: If you scored *three or above* in this section, the impact your toxic boss is having on your work is significant and your self-confidence is being damaged. You don't deserve to feel this way—and you don't have to. Continuing to do the exercises in this book will help you to make a plan to regain your confidence and control of your career. Also, it may be time to do something about your state of mind by seeking support and guidance from a professional or mentor who can help you regain your belief in yourself.

If you checked *any* of these five items, your belief in your abilities has been impacted by your work situation. This is not acceptable, as your self-confidence and self-esteem are crucial to your career growth and success. Take some time to reflect by answering these questions in your journal:

1. How long have you been feeling this lower self-confidence?
2. What are the risks to your work if these feelings continue?
3. What are the risks to your well-being if these feelings continue?
4. What is one step you will take to rebuild your self-confidence? (*Note: You will learn about various strategies for your recovery later in this book.*)

TOXIC BOSS WORK IMPACT #2: DETACHMENT AND DISENGAGEMENT FROM WORK

- ❑ I've been feeling disengaged and disconnected from my work
- ❑ I no longer feel invested in my job
- ❑ I've been losing the passion or enthusiasm I used to have for my work
- ❑ I no longer feel committed to the organization
- ❑ I've been feeling checked out, like I'm just going through the motions

TOTAL: ________ /5

WHAT YOUR SCORE MEANS:

The higher your score in this section, the more you're feeling disengaged and detached from work, and your toxic boss is likely the biggest reason you're feeling that way.

If you checked any of these five items, your engagement with your job is suffering. Lower engagement can ultimately affect your performance and commitment to your work. If you checked one or more items, take some time to reflect by answering these questions in your journal:

1. When was the last time you felt engaged in your work?
2. How is feeling detached and disengaged impacting your work? (e.g., your efficiency, accuracy, or quality of work)
3. What are the risks to your life if you continue to feel disengaged in this way?
4. What type of work environment would feel engaging for you?

TOXIC BOSS WORK IMPACT #3: MOTIVATION

- ❑ I'm no longer motivated to do my best work
- ❑ I've lost my sense of ambition
- ❑ I've been coasting and doing the bare minimum
- ❑ I'm no longer willing to do anything extra
- ❑ I've been feeling apathetic about my work

TOTAL: _________ /5

WHAT YOUR SCORE MEANS:

The higher your score in this section, the more you're feeling demotivated in your work. If these feelings are because of your toxic boss, it's time to be fully aware.

If you checked any of these five items, your work motivation is suffering. Lower motivation can ultimately affect your performance and success at work. Know that you deserve to be in a role and work environment that motivate you. If you checked one or more of these items, take some time to reflect by answering these questions in your journal:

1. How is feeling demotivated impacting your work? (e.g., your ability to meet deadlines or the quality of your deliverables)
2. What are the risks of continuing to feel demotivated? (e.g., potentially losing your job or not getting a good raise or bonus)
3. What type of workplace and leader would help re-motivate you?

TOXIC BOSS WORK IMPACT #4: PERFORMANCE AND PRODUCTIVITY

- ❑ I've been feeling less productive
- ❑ I haven't been meeting my deadlines
- ❑ I've been making more mistakes
- ❑ I'm not working efficiently (due to so much energy being put into navigating my boss)
- ❑ I've been taking more sick days than usual

TOTAL: _________ /5

WHAT YOUR SCORE MEANS:

The higher your score in this section, the more your performance and productivity are being negatively impacted by your toxic boss.

If you didn't check any of these items, it's good to know that you're still performing well in your work, despite having a toxic boss. This is no small feat! But stay aware of these potential impacts on your productivity and watch out for these warning signs of decreased performance and productivity.

Warning: If you scored *three or above* in this section, you may be at risk of being let go due to your decreased work quality and reliability. If you checked one or more of these five items, your work performance is suffering. And any impacts on your work performance are important to be aware of, as these can impact your career growth and progression. Take some time to reflect by answering these questions in your journal:

1. How important is it to me to leave on my own terms versus being fired or laid off?
2. Are there aspects of my work that I want to improve while navigating my broader plan forward?
3. What type of workplace and leader do I perform best for? (e.g., What type of work environment would I thrive in? What are the qualities I value in a boss?)
4. When was the last time I was in a position where I was performing successfully, and how can I get to that place again?

Hopefully, these four mini-quizzes have given you valuable insight into the detrimental impact your toxic boss is having on your work. You can use your results to help inform your decision-making going forward.

YOUR TOTAL "TOXIC BOSS WORK IMPACTS" SCORE: Now add up your total score for the items you checked across the previous four mini-checklists for Toxic Boss Impacts #1–#4 (for a maximum of 20 points). Your total score will allow you to determine where the impacts on your work fall in these categories:

Red Alarm Zone—More than 10 out of 20: Your toxic boss is significantly impacting your work and you need to make an exit plan immediately, or risk being set free without having a plan in place. Feeling bad about your work abilities, disengaged, demotivated, and not performing at your best is no way to live; you deserve better, and the coming chapters will help you create a more positive path forward, so read on.

Given your high score, it may be helpful to get additional supports (e.g., a career psychologist, counselor, coach, or mentor) to help you navigate your next steps and rebuild your feelings of motivation and confidence so you can perform at your best. Searching for psychologists, counselors, or coaches that specialize in career and workplace challenges in your location would be a great place to start.

High Risk Zone—5–10 out of 20: Your toxic boss is starting to impact your work, and being aware of this as you navigate your next steps will be critical. There's a risk of these impacts growing as your toxic boss continues to damage your ability to feel and be effective in your work. Now is the time to begin thinking about how you can find a position that will reenergize and motivate you to perform at your best.

Moderate Risk Zone—1–4 out of 20: Although you checked very few items, it's still important that you reflect on these areas and take action to improve your situation. Even a single item on this checklist can impact your work effectiveness and belief in yourself. Think about what *is* in your control and whether there is a way to address these aspects in the short term. You may want to consider planning for your exit before things get worse; or, if you choose to stay, start working now on setting boundaries as best you can and taking care of your well-being.

So, What Are Your Options?

The urgency with which you should take action to change your situation relates directly to whether you're in the Red Alarm, High Risk, or Moderate Risk Zones previously described. If you're in the Red Alarm or High Risk Zones, taking action quickly will be critical for your well-being.

Regardless of your score and how stuck you feel, you *do* have options. Your career is yours to lead, and although you may have lost control due to your toxic boss, you *can* regain that control. (We will discuss this concept of proactively managing your career journey going forward in greater detail in Chapter 7.)

It may be helpful as you explore your options to imagine your career as a car, and your toxic boss as a hijacker who has firmly planted themself in the driver's seat. Know that you can take back control of that car by becoming the driver once again. Your career path is yours alone, and is a precious gift in this evolving world. You *deserve* to be in a career that allows you to use your talents, be respected, and feel good about your contributions.

Remember that when we're under the duress of a toxic boss our imagination may become limited by a combination of stress and lack of self-confidence, leaving us unable to consider the possibilities ahead in an optimistic, or even *realistic*, manner. As one of my research participants explained, "It's almost impossible, when you are in the thick of it, to envision a realistic next phase. So the actual outcome always ends up better than what you could possibly have imagined as a best-case scenario at the time."

I've had countless people sit across from me in career counseling sessions worried that they'll never be able to find fulfillment in their career. They are really good at "yes, but . . ." statements like:

- *"Yes, there may be opportunities to make as much money in another industry, but in my case I'm just not going to find something that gives me the same overall comp package."*
- *"Switching jobs may be an option, but with the economy the way it is, I'm trapped in this horrible situation."*
- *"There may be other opportunities out there, but now that I'm in my mid-fifties, employers think I'm too old and would rather have younger talent."*

Hundreds of people I've personally seen in this state have, after doing the work to get back in control of their career, ended up landing in much better and healthier positions at work. They often reach out months or years later to thank me for believing in them when they didn't believe in themselves and sharing how much better things are going for them now that they're in a healthier workplace.

You're reading this book for a reason, and I believe you can do this too! Consider each of the following options as you choose the road onto which you'd like to steer your career car. Note the pros and cons of each option in your journal.

Option 1: Stick It Out for Now

Anil felt his blood boil when he pulled into the office parkade. He resented another day having to work for his toxic boss. Whatever he designed today would be picked apart

100 times over, so what was the point? This was beyond micromanagement; it was his boss fully redoing his job on a daily basis.

Anil had thought about quitting many times, but his family depended on his income, and he had a sizable pension that he had worked for decades to build and would lose if he quit. So, despite the daily temptation of leaving, he was resigned to sticking it out.

Hopefully his boss would retire soon. There had been rumors of that for a few years now. On the other hand, he'd heard his boss brag before that he would rule their department until his last breath.

Anil pursed his lips as he pressed the elevator button to his floor, wondering how he was going to endure many more months, or even years, working under this jerk.

If leaving your job does not feel like a viable option, you can try to set boundaries or change your mindset while continuing to work for your toxic boss. To be honest, I have rarely seen this strategy work in a situation with a truly toxic boss. This strategy *can* work well if yours is a difficult boss, as defined earlier in this book, as difficult bosses can be managed. When it comes to *toxic* bosses, however, the persistence and severity of their behaviors toward you make it difficult to cope regardless of boundary-setting or changed-mindset efforts. That said, if quitting anytime soon is truly not an option, these coping strategies are worth testing to see if they can at least ease the daily grind until you can make a more permanent change to something better in the future.

▸ *Try Setting Boundaries*

You can set boundaries around your work hours, the types of tasks you're being asked to do (e.g., tasks that aren't part of your job description), or unfair or unethical requests your boss is making. For example, you may not volunteer to go pick up muffins for the team meeting after work. Or you may stop checking your work email after normal work hours. Try turning off your phone and shutting down your computer, putting both out of sight so there are no temptations to check in. Also, if possible, try to work remotely as much as you can to create more distance from your toxic boss.

As one of my research participants aptly pointed out, you can use automated tools to help you achieve this (e.g., She once set up a rule in her email software that sent all of her boss's emails to a special folder that she would only check twice a day. This way she wasn't interrupted/thrown off/triggered by her boss's insane tone and constant, overbearing messages).

If your boss has been known to overload you, before agreeing to a new task, make clear that you are already carrying a full load and ask them to let you know which task is a priority. Explain that you're happy to perform the task they're asking you to take on, but if you do prioritize it then something else will need to get bumped. Make it their decision, so they feel in control. Toxic bosses love control.

Many toxic bosses will react negatively to you setting boundaries, particularly if they are a *Control Freak* and your boundaries get in the way of them having full control. Likewise, the *Self-Serving Egomaniac* will not appreciate boundaries that could get in the way of their perceived success. And when it comes to a *Narcissistic* or *Sociopathic* boss, they will definitely not react well to this approach; if you explain that you're overloaded or stressed they will *not* care, as they completely lack empathy. So instead, as a coping strategy, make the boundaries a matter of how you can get their priorities done to make them look good. Stroke their massive egos, as that is the *only* way to navigate these personality disorders.

Just because setting boundaries is difficult with toxic bosses doesn't mean you cannot or should not attempt to do so. You deserve to protect yourself, your reputation, and your time. Just know that this strategy may make things even more challenging with your toxic boss—and remember to document how it goes, tracking your efforts and their responses, so you have some protection if things go sideways.

▸ *Try Shifting Your Mindset*

This is about changing your perspective and focusing on longer-term goals rather than your present situation. Changing your thoughts, perceptions, and interpretations of your current situation can help you better cope under your toxic boss.

An example of changing your perspective is reframing your current brutal situation as a learning experience. As difficult as it may be to find any learnings or positives within your current hell, I challenge you to answer these questions in your journal:

1. How is your toxic boss teaching you what *not* to do as a leader?
2. Has their behavior led you to develop closer bonds with your colleagues, since you're going through it together?
3. Are your efforts to cope with your toxic boss's behavior or assertively set healthy boundaries helping you develop greater resiliency?

SHIFTING MINDSET IN ACTION

I would look for joy in helping the business versus helping her. I'd focus on making my team work and feel better and making the rest of the organization work and feel better rather than her.

—DIRECTOR OF AN ENERGY COMPANY

▶ *Try Adjusting Your Psychological Contract*

Beyond your written employment contract, there exists a *psychological contract* between you and your employer. This contract is about the expectations, perceptions, and informal obligations you have, such as being treated fairly and respectfully by your boss. Psychological contracts are subjective and based on each party's interpretations. Your toxic boss has undoubtedly already violated your psychological contract by mistreating you and not supporting you in the ways you expected.

Adjusting your psychological contract as a temporary coping strategy is about changing your expectations and focusing on what you *can* control. For example, by expecting nothing good from your boss and seeing the relationship as purely transactional, you may be able to tolerate them a bit longer. By simultaneously erasing your expectations and bracing yourself for continued toxic behavior, you will spend less of your time being surprised or disappointed. Seeing your current job as merely a paycheck and focusing on your well-being outside of work could help you cope with this situation for longer than will be possible if you allow yourself to feel let down on a daily basis.

I (Dr. Laura) had a toxic boss for a short time after my second maternity leave. The ironic thing was that I had hired her two years before, as I needed a co-manager given our growing team and workload. Then, while I was on leave, she was "promoted" to fully take over management, and I was told I would not be a manager upon returning. The shock and betrayal I felt was tough to process; this was a time in my career I will never forget.

I was now reporting to this woman, who was a challenging combination of arrogant, controlling, and disorganized. She also thought she knew what was best for my career development. Others on the team also found her difficult and frustrating as a manager. I knew I wouldn't be able to last long in that role, as I specialized in leadership development and could not stomach working for a toxic boss.

I did not leave this job right away, but while continuing to work I decided to also teach an undergraduate course in the evenings at a local university that semester. This allowed me to get my mind off work; I found joy in bringing concepts from the real world of work to the students, and in their appreciation of the work I did. This experience allowed me to treat my job more like a job and not go above and beyond, as I no longer had that capacity between my new teaching load and the fact that I had two young sons at home. I had adjusted my psychological contract, and soon after the course I was teaching was done, I quit the job I was no longer enjoying to start my own business.

(As an aside, that toxic boss didn't last long at that organization, either. She ended up leaving to work for a competitor!)

▶ *Practice Self-Care*

Sticking it out with a toxic boss requires prioritizing coping techniques to prevent your physical and mental health from being damaged. These include self-care practices like going for walks in nature, healthy eating, minimizing alcohol and caffeine intake, and exercising. These habits allow you to release the negative energy you've accumulated from dealing with your toxic boss. Further, they build up your energy reserve so that you are better able to handle or bounce back from future toxic behaviors.

Spending time with supportive family and friends is also vital to healing and validating tough experiences with your toxic boss. These relationships help you realize that you are appreciated and valued, and that there's more to your life and identity than your current work situation. Having empathetic support and someone to give you a hug and remind you that things will all work out is fundamental when your confidence and well-being have been depleted by a toxic boss.

Talking with others who have had toxic bosses, or colleagues you can trust at work, can help ground you in knowing that your current experience working for this toxic boss is not your fault—and that there is a way out. Professional resources such as counseling, therapy, and self-help books (like this one!) can also be immensely helpful.

On that note—kudos to you for getting to this point in this book. You're taking important steps in the right direction, and I encourage you to finish so you have the knowledge and techniques at your disposal moving forward.

COPING TECHNIQUES IN ACTION

I have a good husband and we go walking every night after work. We live near a lake and a forest. It's so good to walk in nature. We would talk about my job and my boss every single night. I had to talk about it or I would have had a breakdown.

—BOOKKEEPER, ACCOUNTING FIRM

I was able to negotiate working remotely from another city, which required some courage. This gave me space to begin looking for a job. [My toxic boss] used to just show up at the office unexpectedly and bulldoze . . . so by working remotely, I no longer had to deal with that.

Also, my dog helped me cope on so many levels. I ended up registering her as an emotional support animal. Pets are so therapeutic for stress.

—HEAD OF PRODUCTION

Get some professional validation in the ways that you can. Whether it's through volunteerism or board involvement, seek out different kinds of things that you can do where you can interact with professionals that you respect and that you admire.

—DIRECTOR IN HIGHER EDUCATION

If I didn't have my coworkers there, I would have quit so much sooner, because they were the ones that helped me and gave me lots of positive reinforcement.

—LEGAL ASSISTANT

Ultimately, sticking it out is not a long-term strategy I'd recommend when it comes to a toxic boss. Your well-being and work performance will suffer if you continue under the claws of your toxic boss without an exit plan. After supporting clients through hundreds of instances of toxic boss situations, I see that things tend to change for the worse, despite efforts to stick it out. Remember, one of the top pieces of advice survivors of toxic bosses have to say is, *I wish I'd left sooner.*

Unfortunately, leaving immediately is not a realistic option for many, and it may not be an option for you. Given that you will likely need another job bringing in income before giving your notice, it's a great idea for you to create an exit plan. A well-thought-out exit plan will give you a renewed sense of control of your career and make stepping into a better job much more likely. It will also help you better stomach this situation in the short term.

Option 2: Create Your Exit Plan

Creating an exit plan is a highly recommended step in regaining control of your career. So important, in fact, that the whole next chapter will be dedicated to creating a winning exit plan. There, I'll walk you through how to craft your plan and act on it so that your next opportunity can become a reality sooner rather than later.

Option 3: File a Complaint

Chloe's palms were sweating as she shook hands with the HR manager and was ushered into a private meeting room on a Friday afternoon. She thought about saying this was a mistake, and that she wasn't going to formally file a complaint against her boss. Yet in her heart, she knew it was the right thing to do. Her boss was a bully, and his bullying was not only impacting her but also others on her team. He made derogatory and mean comments, threatened her job by making her feel replaceable, and made sexist and racist comments in team meetings, to name only a few of his horrible behaviors.

The HR manager was professional but warm as Chloe explained the bullying and harassment that had taken place over the past eight months. She assured Chloe that a full investigation would be launched, led by an outside firm, as this was not the first complaint made about this leader. She also promised that the organization would have her back, and that his behavior would be addressed.

Chloe left that meeting room feeling cautiously optimistic. She trusted that HR knew how serious this situation was, and felt relieved that she'd taken this step. She knew she'd done the right thing and hoped she would still have a job the next week . . .

Filing a complaint about your toxic boss is usually done internally, with your organization's HR Department. Depending on the size and sophistication of your organization, there may be a formal mechanism for filing a complaint, or it may simply be done through speaking with your HR advisor. You can start by looking at your organization's code of conduct or respectful workplace policy, and find out if avenues for filing complaints are included. Depending on your toxic boss's behaviors, the complaint may fall under harassment or bullying.

Although the hope is that taking this step will get your organization to investigate and deal with your toxic boss, for the employees I have interviewed and worked with, this was the exception and not the rule. Despite their best intentions to help you, HR is part of your organization's hierarchy and they may not have the power to set an investigation of your boss in motion. If they do have the influence and ability to launch an investigation or to have your toxic boss given a warning or performance management plan via their boss, however, that's great news.

Keep in mind, for this path to be successful, your boss must report to someone who:

1. Cares about people at all levels of the organization and treats toxic behaviors seriously.
2. Has the courage to address these concerns and have difficult conversations.
3. Has a professional relationship and clear boundaries, versus being buddies with your toxic boss.

If any of these conditions are not met, it is very unlikely that your toxic boss's supervisor will be an ally to you or HR in addressing their bad behavior.

In some cases, HR will go to your boss with your concerns. This can make your situation more uncomfortable in the short term, and potentially even worse longer term. To protect yourself as much as possible, always:

1. Ask HR what the process is, especially what constitutes a complaint and what protections you can expect.
2. Confirm the confidentiality of your discussion/complaint.
3. Request a written follow-up from HR confirming your complaint or, if preferable, an overview of your conversation (this should include a commitment that you will be free from reprisals).

4. Follow up with a written request that you would like to be kept informed of any communications that may further impact your working relationship with your boss.

Remember, HR is not independent from the political landscape in your organization and is under the direction of higher-ups who may or may not have the courage or consider addressing toxic leadership to be a priority.

Proving that your boss's behavior is damaging and goes against the code of conduct and/or respectful workplace policy of your organization requires documented examples of behaviors, which often requires a workplace investigation. Statements from those who have observed/witnessed or themselves experienced your toxic boss's behaviors are key, but sometimes others are afraid to put themselves out there, for fear of losing their jobs.

This is not to say you shouldn't consider filing a complaint, or that you shouldn't trust your HR team. There are many dedicated HR leaders who will go to great lengths to address toxic leadership and put their own positions at risk to do so. But do your due diligence: Make sure you understand the process, policies, and your rights. Be clear on what outcome you are hoping for (such as your boss being transferred or fired). Decide up front what level of risk and time commitment you are willing to make in this regard (how long are you willing to hang on until a change is made?). And lastly, find the level where your complaint may make a difference, and explore whether other complaints have been successfully addressed in the organization.

Sometimes complaints do lead to positive outcomes, such as your boss getting fired—especially if they've had other complaints filed against them and yours is the final straw in a long lineup of issues. Another outcome is that your boss may have their leadership responsibilities pulled away but remain in the organization due to their experience, connections, or technical expertise. So long as you don't have to interact or collaborate with them regularly, this solution can work out positively for you too.

In sum, having a strong and trusting relationship with your HR leader or advisor can help your cause. Filing a complaint takes courage, but make sure you weigh the pros and cons, as well as your risk tolerance. Determine if the stress and risk of filing a complaint are worth it, or if a fresh start somewhere else makes more sense. Think of it as a "fight or flight" decision—are you more drawn to escaping or fighting against your toxic boss?

Trust your gut and listen to the cues from your workplace to help you determine if fight or flight is the best path for *you*.

FILING TOXIC BOSS COMPLAINTS IN ACTION

My HR advisor was there for me every step of the way. Others had also complained about this toxic boss, and my complaint led to a full investigation and to their termination in the weeks that followed.

—COMMERCIAL PROPERTY MANAGER

It got back to my boss [that I'd filed a complaint] and I was let go, even though HR put in writing I wouldn't get fired if I came forward. Anything I told HR got back to my boss.

—DIRECTOR IN HEALTHCARE

Option 4: Take Legal Action

Stanley's thoughts had been all over the place. He was obsessing over whether he should take legal action against his employer and toxic boss, or just put this phase of his life behind him. He was burnt out, feeling exhausted and more cynical about work than he had ever felt. His emotions were a roller coaster of hurt, anger, and resentment. After speaking with a reputable employment lawyer, he was confident he had a case—but was a legal battle where he wanted to spend his energy?

Zuri was exhausted from the past eighteen months of fighting against her former toxic boss, a deceitful snake who constantly played games to impact her work. Her boss would change direction on a project suddenly without informing Zuri, then reprimand her for going in the wrong direction. She also made efforts to pit Zuri's colleagues against her, creating a cutthroat work environment.

Zuri had filed a civil lawsuit after taking a medical leave when she could no longer endure the harassment, dishonesty, manipulation, and gross unfairness at her job. Her career progress had been thwarted and her physical and mental health harmed. Yet she had fought for what was just and fair, and winning her case was a feeling she would never forget. Justice had prevailed, and her settlement would not only cover her legal bills but also provide her with funds to give her the flexibility to pivot to a much healthier organization.

Taking legal action against a toxic boss is a huge decision, and there is no right or wrong answer. It's a very personal decision. Informing yourself about your rights as an employee is a key step on your toxic-boss journey. If you are unionized or represented by an association, reaching out to them as a member is your best first step. Otherwise, consulting an employment lawyer can help you learn how to best protect yourself and what possible legal actions you could take now or later.

Filing a legal or human rights complaint may be an option to consider, depending on:

- The severity of your situation and the level of abuse you're experiencing
- If you cannot afford to be fired/laid off or to leave (e.g., you have significant equity, tenure, or pension tied to the organization)
- The extent to which your toxic boss is impacting your financial situation (e.g., withholding bonuses or raises you clearly deserved, without a fair rationale)
- If HR cannot help

Although this book will help you as you navigate what's best for you going forward, it cannot replace also seeking legal advice if you're looking to fully understand whether you might have a case and what the process would involve. The legal channels and court processes for this differ depending on where you are located. Ask around your network about trusted employment lawyers in your region if you are considering these options to determine if you have a viable case. Nothing beats a solid word-of-mouth recommendation.

These options take courage and resilience, as they are usually emotionally demanding and can drag on for a long period of time. Journal about the costs/benefits and ensure that you have lots of good family and friend support if you do choose this path. Winning a claim against a toxic boss takes great courage and stamina. It can also be incredibly psychologically and financially rewarding—but the legal journey is not for everyone, and determining whether you are equipped to expend the emotional and financial costs of seeking justice is something only you can do.

Option 5: Take a Leave

Larissa walked out of the office that Tuesday with her shoulders slumped. She felt utterly depleted and could no longer hold off her tears; she'd already had to retreat to the restroom a few times that day to hide her distress.

As she tried to focus on the report, her mind kept getting in the way. Why was she not stronger? Sure, her boss had been abusive, manipulative, and ultra-controlling, but Larissa knew she was more intelligent than him. Further, she had always had the stamina to weather storms in her career. But this storm felt like too much. She was at the end of her rope and felt like she was drowning.

The idea of taking a leave had been floated to her by various friends and family, but she had refused to take a leave because she thought it would be career suicide. After this day, though, she finally succumbed and went to her doctor, who gave her a letter recommending she take a three-month medical leave. She immediately submitted this letter to HR, asking them to inform her immediate supervisor, as she could not face doing so herself.

As she exited the front doors of the building into the crisp fall air, Larissa knew she would not be back any time soon, and perhaps not ever.

In most countries, a paid (or partially paid, depending on the health insurance plan parameters of the employer and the country's laws) leave can be arranged to take time off your job for medical reasons, including mental health. Many people fear that taking a medical leave will jeopardize their job and security with their employer. But medical leaves are more common today than they were in the past, and if you're burned out or suffering health impacts from the stress of your toxic boss, a medical leave may be just the option you need.

The benefit of taking a leave is the time it allows you to focus on recovering both your mental and physical health. It also gives you the time and space away from your toxic boss you need to be able to see the situation more fully than is possible when you're entrenched in the daily grind. After a leave, you can return with clearer strategies for boundaries and protecting your well-being, or with a timeline for your exit plan.

Many people decide not to return to reporting to their toxic boss after a leave, as they realize going back is simply not a healthy option. In addition to healing, they use some of this time to figure out their next career move and work on landing their next position.

TAKING A LEAVE IN ACTION

A leave can provide you with respite if you are caught in a self-fulfilling catch-22 where the abuse is impacting your performance and likely to give your toxic boss ammunition to punish or fire you. In my case, I'd started feeling actual cognitive effects/symptoms like poorer memory, diminished recall, and difficulty with vocabulary . . . it was scary. I knew that if I did not take a leave, I would make the kinds of mistakes I was being falsely accused of making, or lose it in front of my team, or break down, which is exactly what my toxic boss wanted and would have used against me.

—DIRECTOR IN HIGHER EDUCATION

A paid medical leave requires a letter from a healthcare provider that confirms your needs for the leave and a recommended duration. The eligibility criteria and procedures for applying for and being granted a leave will depend on both your employer's policies and the labor laws in your jurisdiction. Unfortunately, not every company or employment situation will have this option.

You can get more information by checking into your health insurance plan as well as speaking confidentially with someone in your Human Resources department. One of my research participants was able to take a mental health leave with the condition that upon returning she would no longer have to report to the same boss. That may not be feasible, depending on your role and the organization, but is worth exploring.

An unpaid leave may be an option you take if your employer and insurance plan do not offer paid medical leave. It puts control of your career back in your hands, but also carries more risk, as there are not as many legal protections in the case of unpaid leaves as there are for medical leaves (i.e., you would be less protected against your employer eliminating your position or from retaliation).

Although you cannot typically be laid off during a medical leave, and doing so upon your return is risky on an employer's part, the potential of being let go can depend on the general toxicity of the organization as well as regional employment laws. A brief consultation with a local employment lawyer can provide clarity on this point. Worker's compensation boards, labor commissions, and/or similar bodies in your jurisdiction should have informational services that counsel individuals in general terms about the law and their rights, often for free.

If you can afford to take some time away from your toxic boss to recover and focus more clearly on your future career planning, perhaps figuring out your next steps so you don't have to return—ever—a leave of absence, whether paid or unpaid, could be an excellent option for you!

Option 6: Enough Is Enough (Quit!)

The option to quit before having another job lined up may become your best option if your mental and physical health is at stake. If you've reached this point in your toxic-boss journey, you simply cannot cope with any more abuse. If you have savings or a partner who can support the bills until you find your next gig, you may be able to bridge your unemployment and not work for a period of time. Or you may find other alternatives may work for you besides seeking another full-time position, such as working for yourself, starting a business, or contracting.

It may also be worth it to double-check the unemployment insurance conditions in your jurisdiction. Although you normally can't claim unemployment insurance if you quit, there sometimes exists a special process if employers make it impossible for you to stay. And depending on your situation, it may also be worth negotiating terms with HR (e.g., can they declare you terminated instead of resigned so you can get unemployment insurance?). In this case, you are not officially filing a complaint but you are flagging to HR the reasons for your exit, and they may want to protect themselves by allowing you to be terminated instead of quitting.

Before quitting, make sure you have a clear sense of your financial runway. Dipping into your savings can be worth it if you're doing so in return for regaining your health and well-being. I can attest that many who do leave move into jobs under healthy bosses where they not only thrive emotionally but also actually earn more.

Consider speaking to your financial planner and bank to figure out a plan before officially pulling the plug so you can answer these types of questions for yourself:

- How long can you survive without your paycheck? (taking into account what your final pay will be, including any vacation pay you've accrued that will get paid out)
- Which of your savings or investments would make sense to cash out to sustain you until your next job?
- If you need additional credit, or to pull from an existing line of credit, how will this work and how can you minimize any interest you incur?

In your analysis of the cost of leaving, don't forget to consider the cost of staying. For example, your toxic boss may be limiting your career development and pay, the costs of which add up over time and can be far more than a period of unemployment.

ENOUGH IS ENOUGH IN ACTION

My long-term goals were keeping me going, but at some point, I just kind of broke. This isn't the way that you treat people and this isn't the way that I should have to feel.

—ADMINISTRATOR TO AN ELECTED OFFICIAL

There's a lot of lessons learned. But I tell you, overall, it's good being out of there and it's much healthier being out of there. I feel like I gained ten years back of my life. I felt like I was a prisoner of war working there.

—DIRECTOR IN HEALTHCARE

Exploring your alternatives can help you take back control of your career as you ultimately decide the best path forward. You should now have a clearer sense of the option or options that make the most sense for your scenario, and have the tools to start exploring your next steps. The next chapter on creating a winning exit plan will help you continue to plan for a much better future work situation.

Takeaways from Chapter 3

- ✓ Toxic bosses impact your effectiveness in your work.
- ✓ Your confidence, engagement, motivation, productivity, and performance can all suffer under a toxic boss.
- ✓ There are six main options when it comes to your next steps with your toxic boss.
- ✓ Sticking it out may involve setting boundaries, shifting your mindset, adjusting your psychological contract, and putting into place coping techniques.
- ✓ Creating your exit plan includes determining your timeline and beginning your internal and/or external job search.
- ✓ Filing a complaint often involves your HR department or legal avenues, and carries both benefits and risks.
- ✓ There are various options for legal action, and those are best discussed with a recommended employment lawyer in your region.

✓ Taking a paid or unpaid leave can be an option for recovering your health and examining your situation more fully.

✓ Deciding to leave without another job in place may be an option when you've simply had enough and the health risks outweigh the job security (and you can bridge your unemployment financially).

CHAPTER 4:

CREATING A WINNING EXIT PLAN

"Bad leadership is an invisible plague that affects everyone."
—John C. Maxwell

Allan's wife always brought up how miserable he was at his job on Sunday evenings, and each time she begged him to start looking seriously for another job. She was worried about his high blood pressure and knew that his Abusive A-Hole boss was stressing him out constantly.

Every time they had this conversation, Allan would promise that this week he was going to start looking—that he would reach out to his network and check out job postings. But every day he had an excuse for not following through—like having to work in the evening, business travel, wanting to chill on the sofa, or being too tired. Their Sunday night conversation felt like a broken record.

Allan had no exit plan, nor the motivation to create one. Weeks turned into months, and the reality that Allan might never leave his toxic situation felt increasingly bleak.

An exit plan is a strategy for how and in what timeframe you will leave your current job and toxic boss. Creating an exit plan is a critical step toward regaining a sense of control and a healthier path forward in your career and life once you've made the decision to leave your job. The following steps will help you craft a winning exit plan that will propel you forward with greater confidence and energy.

The alternative to having a clear exit plan is to wing it, letting things unfold as they may. The problem with winging it when you have a toxic boss is that things *will* get worse, and your energy and confidence will continue to deplete over time, making exiting more challenging farther down the road.

Avoiding a situation like Allan's requires executing a clear exit plan. Consider the case of Paula, who, unlike Allan, found a way to formulate an exit plan:

Paula was at her wits' end with her toxic boss. She had taken my quiz (the one from Chapter 2) to determine what persona(s) best described her toxic boss, and it was now clear that her boss was a Self-Serving Egomaniac, a Dishonest Manipulator, and an Abusive A-Hole.

Nearly every morning, Paula would promise herself she'd start looking for another job—but by the time she finished her workday, she'd be so exhausted or emotional that the idea of getting onto her laptop to search for jobs in the evening seemed impossible. Her boss's behavior was getting worse each week and she knew she needed to get out, but she couldn't just quit. She needed a comparable salary to keep paying her bills.

A good friend stopped by her condo with a gift one Saturday afternoon. "Paula," she said, "I've never seen you this unhappy and stressed at work. I wanted to bring you this to help."

Paula was touched as she pulled the crinkly tissue from the gift bag to reveal a small whiteboard and a journal. Written on the whiteboard in black marker was a message from her friend: "Please write your exit date here and put me in a spot where you will see me daily." She hugged her friend, moved to tears by her thoughtful gesture.

"The journal is for you to map out your exit plan with things you will do each week to make it happen," her friend explained. "I will be here to support you, Paula, and I know you can get away from your horrible boss! One step at a time."

This interaction gave Paula a renewed energy. She went on to set a three-month "good riddance" date and complete the steps needed to find another job. Sure, some days she was less motivated than others—but seeing the exit date on her whiteboard each day and journaling regularly propelled her to make daily and weekly actions a reality . . . and by the time those three months expired, she had landed a new and much healthier job.

The steps we'll go over in this chapter will outline how to craft this plan so that you can leave your toxic boss in a realistic and motivating timeline.

Step 1: Determine Your Timeline

Having an exit date that you write down and keep in mind is an important step toward taking back control of your career and life. A motivating way to refer to this is a *Good Riddance* (GR) date. A GR date helps you imagine the relief of sending in your resignation and never having to report to your toxic boss for another day of work. Committing to a timeline for yourself will give you the sense of hope and renewed energy you need to make your next job opportunity a reality.

How far away you set your date will depend on the variables in your situation. For the majority of people, the financial concerns around leaving are paramount. Factors that need to be carefully examined may include:

1. Financial incentives, such as an upcoming bonus or a pension that has not yet vested, that you're waiting on.
2. Your personal financial situation, which may include considerations like:
    a. Do you have savings you could tap into to give you more time to job hunt should you still not have a new role by your exit date?
    b. Do you have a partner who earns an income and is able to carry the bills for a period if needed?
3. The market conditions in your industry, such as:
    a. Are there lots of jobs available in your industry and at your level?
    b. Is the economy currently experiencing a downturn, with fewer job prospects and lots of layoffs happening?

In general, a realistic GR date should be three to six months away, at a maximum. Why do I recommend this timeline? Because every month working under a toxic boss is increasingly harmful to your well-being, and this timeline allows space to search for alternatives without leaving room for procrastination. Setting a timeline too far out (beyond six months) leads to delaying job search activities, whereas setting a timeline too soon (shorter than three months) is unrealistic and stressful.

When setting your GR date, consider the time of year as quieter job search periods, like holidays or summer, may impact your timeline.

I strongly recommend running your timeline by trusted friends, colleagues, or loved ones who have your best interests at heart. Over and over, I've seen people set their timeline further out than they need to, and in doing so subject themselves to unnecessary suffering. This is normal, but resist the urge. Be open to hearing what others you trust are saying about your timeframe and opportunities, to balance any fear-based thoughts you are having. Of course, it's ultimately your decision, and the timeline you're comfortable with is important, but when working for a toxic boss, your judgment and confidence will be clouded and based more in emotion and fear than reality and possibility.

Interestingly, many of my research participants emphasized that thinking about their exit plan in months rather than years was essential. As one participant, a director at a post-secondary institution, put it, "You will have fear about making the leap." Feeling afraid of this change is normal; you are not alone. But is that fear preventing you from thinking through solutions in a hope-filled manner? Consider the difference between these two examples:

Fear-based ruminations

- *I will not be able to find an equivalent job, and all my hard work and experience will go down the drain.*

- *I have no time to look for work, only a little on weekends, so it's going to take me more than a year to get out, if I'm lucky.*
- *The market is bad right now, so I'm going to be stuck here for a long time.*
- *Now that I'm older, my prospects are limited, and ageism will prevent me from getting a good job.*

Hope-based thinking

- *I don't know what's out there, but I trust there are options I haven't even thought of.*
- *Although I will lose some of my pension if I leave this year, I can think of a few ways I can counterbalance that loss by considering the following:*
    - *Are there entrepreneurial gigs I'd enjoy that would allow me to make up the difference over time?*
    - *Can I find a job with a compensation package that will make up the difference I'll lose in pension if I leave?*
- *It may take longer to find a job in this market, but if I start now and put in four hours a week, I will make progress toward a much better fit.*
- *With my age, I bring a lot of experience, and people are working well into their seventies these days, so being in my fifties means I have twenty more years of career left to contribute my knowledge in healthier settings!*

How did reading the fear-based thinking versus the hope-based thinking examples feel for you? If hope-based thinking feels too difficult right now, enlist a loved one or trusted friend or colleague who is an optimistic person to support and challenge your thinking. Share your fear-based thoughts and ask them to help you turn them into more hope-filled ones. It's also valuable to journal your fear-based thoughts and practice challenging each of these yourself.

In sum, setting a realistic timeline—in months, not years—will allow for you to make your leap in a carefully planned way for a brighter future. Although your timeline may change due to unforeseen hurdles, such as your job prospects and labor market conditions, having a GR date is important for you to see the light at the end of this dark, toxic-boss tunnel. Your GR date will help propel you to do your part by taking the necessary actions to make your exit a reality.

(**Note:** Between now and your GR date, be sure to put into place the coping techniques under *Option 1: Stick It Out for Now* in Chapter 3. These include setting boundaries as best you can, shifting your mindset, and self-care practices, which are critical to preserving your well-being during the remainder of your toxic boss reporting relationship.)

Dr. Laura's Coaching Break: *Setting a realistic and healthy GR date*

Ask yourself the following questions and write the answers in your journal:

1. What is a realistic timeframe for exiting this toxic scenario (my GR date)?
2. Have I run my timeline by trusted friends, colleagues, or loved ones?
3. Is my timeline too heavily based in fear versus hope? How so?

4. Write out some of the recurring thoughts you are having, whether fear-based or hope-based. Underline or highlight your hope-based thoughts.
5. Who can be a hopeful voice to encourage me along the way and refute my fear-based thoughts?

Note: If you find yourself constantly stuck in your head or completely overwhelmed, anxious, or unable to self-motivate despite trying all these strategies, then consider reaching out to a career counselor, psychologist, or coach who can help guide you through these steps and offer objective advice on your skills and fit for various opportunities.

Step 2: Keep Your Battery Charged

As you are working on and executing your exit plan, you will need more energy, so you'll also need a plan to nurture your physical and mental health. This requires taking the time to do things that rebuild your energy. Think of your body (including your brain) as a rechargeable battery that needs to be replenished daily. The more energy you can rebuild, the more your job search will gain momentum.

As we discussed in Chapter 1, working for a toxic boss is emotionally and physically depleting. Your energy will often be drained by navigating your toxic boss, which will make focusing on your job search even more difficult. Creating a personal wellness plan with daily things that you can do to replenish your energy, however small they may be, can go a long way toward helping you build your energy levels.

I coach my clients to think in terms of these domains of their well-being:

- Physical activity/fitness (e.g., walks, exercise classes, yoga, etc.)
- Mindfulness (e.g., meditation apps, journaling, deep breathing techniques)
- Connection (e.g., coffee with a friend, a supportive call with a trusted family member)
- Nutrition (e.g., healthy food, avoiding alcohol or too much caffeine, lots of water)
- Sleep (e.g., consistent bedtime routine, getting support from a sleep doctor or specialist if needed)
- Spirituality (e.g., gratitude practice, spiritual books or readings, YouTube videos, prayer, spiritual communities)

This is just a small sampling of examples from each of these categories; there are so many more available to you, and the combination of self-care methods you choose to focus on will be personal and unique to you. In Chapter 6: Recovering from a Toxic Boss, I will dive into more detail on this front.

Dr. Laura's Coaching Break: *Keeping your battery charged with a personal wellness plan*

In your journal or an electronic document, create a table for your personal wellness plan. The table will have your wellness categories in column 1. The way you will name and order these is up to you. Start with a table like the following example:

MY PERSONAL WELLNESS PLAN			
Wellness Categories	Monday	Tuesday	Wednesday
	Activity	*Activity*	*Activity*
Physical			
Mindful			
Connection			
Nutrition			
Sleep			
Spiritual			

MY PERSONAL WELLNESS PLAN			
Thursday	Friday	Saturday	Sunday
Activity	*Activity*	*Activity*	*Activity*

As you can see, the remaining days of the week will be listed in the other columns, and in the cells will be each of the activities you will do within each category over the following week. You will *not* have time to tackle all categories in one day, so space out your activities so you cover all categories over the course of a week.

Note that some categories will have more activities than others. For example, staying active, even if that means a short walk, is a key aspect of well-being, so try to do something physically active on at least four to five of the seven days in your plan. Mindfulness and/or spirituality are practices best done daily, but if you are new to these then start small, with even a couple of times per week at first, and grow from there. Connection means different things to different people, so spacing and pacing your time with others will vary greatly between individuals, but we all can benefit from at least some social connection during a difficult period like this one.

You will update this plan one week at a time, then reflect on how the activities you engaged in served you and make adjustments for the following week. I recommend mapping out the week and weekend to come on Sundays, but it's up to you which day you do so; the main thing is consistency and following through.

The following portion of a weekly personal wellness plan is an example, to get you thinking about how this strategy could specifically look for *you*. Try not to over plan, as you'll need rest days (physically in particular), and you don't want to get overwhelmed and end up ignoring your plan altogether. *Less is more* when you're getting started. It's okay not to fill out all of the cells.

Once you've tested your plan, you can capture your *weekly wisdom* at the end of each week by journaling how these activities went and how each one made you feel. Be kind to yourself

MY PERSONAL WELLNESS PLAN			
Wellness Categories	Monday	Tuesday	Wednesday
	Activity	*Activity*	*Activity*
Physical	Yoga class	Rest day	Walk
Mindful	Meditation app, journal		Meditation app, journal
Connection	Coffee with friend		Dinner out with spouse
Nutrition	Eat pre-prepared healthy meals; avoid alcohol	Eat pre-prepared healthy meals; avoid alcohol	Make healthy choice at restaurant; limit to one alcoholic drink, then herbal tea
Sleep	Follow bedtime routine; goal 8 hours	Follow bedtime routine; goal 8 hours	Follow bedtime routine; goal 8 hours
Spiritual	Intentions and affirmations	Read chapter of spiritual book before bed	

as you review how your week went, and don't worry if you didn't do everything you planned. It's about progress, not perfection; it's about the things you *do* get around to doing, not about the things you *didn't* do.

Answer the following questions in your journal:

1. What went well with my wellness plan this past week?
2. What wellness practices best renewed my energy?
3. What did I learn about myself and how to recharge my battery?

4. What got in the way of certain activities and how can I hold that space more firmly next week?
5. What supports or accountability partners can help me make these habits a reality (e.g., a good friend, spouse, coach, etc.)?

Step 3: Begin Your Job Search

Finding another position is often a necessary step before quitting a toxic boss. You may want a similar job or you may feel ready for something different; working under a toxic boss will make you feel dissatisfied overall, so it may be confusing to know whether you should find a different career path altogether, or if doing the same type of job under a better boss is the answer.

Given the churn of emotions and thoughts you are dealing with, changing careers altogether will take some time and mental space. But suffering under a toxic boss leaves you with less energy to think and work through a career change, so you may need to prioritize changing jobs if you don't have the ability to quit. Once you're settled and in a better space emotionally and mentally, you can take time to figure out your next career steps. (Note that working with a career counselor or career psychologist at that point can be very beneficial. Working with people who are in a headspace to proactively figure out their career path is a great part of the work I do.)

Internal vs. External Searches

In some organizations, particularly if they are large enough, there may be the chance to network for or apply to other jobs internally. Depending on your toxic boss's job level, network, and span of control, this may or may not feel like a feasible option for you. Some toxic bosses make it impossible to move within an organization, their ballooned egos thwarting any employee's attempt to escape their influence. But before discounting this option altogether, it's worth considering potential options within the company you're with now, especially if you like the organization and culture in general or if the job market in your location is challenging.

When it comes to searching for jobs externally, the most common barrier to success is a lack of energy or confidence. Both have been depleted by your toxic boss, which is why your exit plan includes your personal wellness. Your energy may be sapped by the end of your workdays, and the thought of squeezing in a job search might be overwhelming. This is why the previous section on keeping your battery charged is so key.

Start with small steps, setting bite-size goals and tasks that gradually move you forward. Searching for a job can be overwhelming, but approaching it as a step-by-step process—taking one small action at a time—can help make it more manageable. Some people can slot in job-search activities before or after their workday, or even during their lunch hour. Other people prefer doing most of their search activity on the weekend, or even taking periodic days off to focus on what needs to get done.

Don't search for work during your current job's work time. This will impact your productivity and potentially cause further challenges with your toxic boss, whether or not you get caught. Plus, it's not fair to search for other employment during company time, and doing so often becomes a slippery slope that causes more stress than it's ultimately worth.

Steps to Get You Going

Whether you'll be searching for another role internally or externally, getting yourself ready to showcase your skills and experience will increase your chances of success. The three key job search components, which you can tackle one at a time, are your resume, your online professional presence (e.g., LinkedIn), and your cover letter.

If you haven't updated your resume in a long time, completing this step can feel daunting. Likewise, if you haven't been regularly using business social media platforms such as LinkedIn, updating your profile and building your network there can seem like an overwhelming task. Again, focusing on one step at a time will make this easier, and the great thing is that each step builds on the next. As your resume improves, your online profile will as well. Highlight similar qualifications, skills, and experiences in both places, and use that new material to inform a great cover letter, which you will need when you begin applying to jobs.

I've trained a national team of career psychologists and job search advisors who have helped thousands of people successfully make the transition to a new job, even in stressful situations like exiting from a toxic workplace. Here's some hot tips to make your search successful:

1. Refresh Your Resume

Update your resume to reflect the type of position you want to be doing moving forward, showcasing your skills and experiences in an easy-to-read way. If certain skills and experiences are no longer relevant or of interest to you in terms of how they might be used in a future job, consider removing these and bolstering the types of experiences you're more interested in attracting.

There are many resources and tips online about resumes you can explore, including sample templates. Perhaps you have a friend or family member who is well versed in helping with resumes whom you can ask for help. There are also experts who can review and help you redesign your resume as needed. Resume review services by career and job search advisors/counselors with this expertise can help you make significant improvements. My team at Canada Career Counselling provides these services, as do providers wherever you're located in the world (for example, Indeed resume services). Clients who get their resumes professionally reviewed stand out in competitive application processes and tend to find jobs sooner.

The biggest problems I see in resumes are:

a. **Too much content (e.g., going back decades with old jobs that don't matter anymore):** This can be overwhelming to review and dilutes the experiences that are most important to your next step.
b. **Not enough white space:** This gives an overwhelmingly cluttered look and feel and makes it difficult for hiring managers to quickly scan for your key skills and experiences.
c. **Not using action verbs:** Beginning each bullet with an action verb (e.g., "managed," "created," "built," "facilitated," etc.) that captures the skills and competencies

of each role will highlight your skills and behaviors in a clear and consistent way.

d. **Errors and mistakes:** Spelling or grammatical errors on resumes sound alarm bells around low attention to detail or lack of care.

2. Polish Your Online Professional Presence

When you search your own name online, what comes up? Prospective employers will often do this search to see what they can find. I recommend making your personal social media accounts private, so that only your professional presence is found in such a search, and to update your professional profiles wherever they exist, including on job boards like Indeed.

The current most used professional networking and job search platform is LinkedIn, so keeping your profile up to date there is critical. LinkedIn is important for both networking and job searching, and employers *do* look for talent there regularly. You should update your paid and volunteer roles, including your present position, and ensure you're regularly building connections and expanding your network on the site. Every time I meet someone at an event or training, I ask to connect with them on LinkedIn—and now, as a result of that practice, I have thousands in my network. LinkedIn is a gift for your job search, allowing you to find connections as they move around so you're better able to leverage your network when you need it. Showcasing your best, professional self there is important, whether or not you're actively searching for a new job.

Depending on your industry, there may be certain networking platforms that are more widely used than LinkedIn. For example, in some industries, Facebook groups exist for networking purposes. You will also want to explore industry association platforms and alumni groups, as well as niche recruiters in your space.

Note: If you're still working for your toxic boss when you start your search, you'll need to be discreet . . . don't signal that you're searching for another job publicly. You don't want your toxic boss to find out you're leaving until you're ready to discuss your departure. In the meantime, you *can* be active on job search platforms without declaring publicly that you're looking for a job, so don't put this off. Focus on creating a professional and compelling profile and making as many meaningful connections as possible, privately messaging or applying where and when it's worth doing so.

Remember that on certain platforms, such as LinkedIn, you can adjust your privacy settings to avoid a broadcast of changes to your profile. For example, it's a good idea to set your "open to work" section of LinkedIn to be viewable by recruiters only. Also, following the pages of companies you'd like to work for on LinkedIn and setting up job alerts so you can see when they are hiring is a useful, more passive strategy.

Of course, there's always a small risk of your job search getting back to your toxic boss, should they be connected in some way to a person at the organization you're applying to, but use your judgment. Consider how you would respond to your toxic boss if you were confronted about this and devise a strategy in advance. Only you can decide what level of risk is worth taking as you navigate your search, so think that through up front.

3. Update Your Cover Letter

Although it's easier to submit the same resume over and over to job postings, crafting a tailored cover letter will set you apart and enable you to draw connections between your skills and the specific requirements of the position.

A well-written and tailored cover letter shows your care and enthusiasm, expressing your desire for the position and showcasing why you are the ideal fit. Employers are more likely to interview people when a well-written cover letter is included with their resume.

Live Networking

Beyond social networking through professional platforms like LinkedIn, *live* networking is still important. "Live" may mean video conversations or in-person meetings with people at organizations you may want to work for, or getting in touch with past colleagues or classmates who may introduce you to potential employers. Make a plan for your networking endeavors. Are there people in your network who you can trust to keep your job search under wraps and would be good to reach out to for a catch-up conversation? These can be people in your organization, in your city, or in other geographies. Schedule a face-to-face conversation or video chat with these individuals.

Too many people spend most of their time applying to online job postings when the much more fruitful way to find a job is through your existing network. Your schedule can fill up quickly with these chats, so I recommend setting a goal that's doable, such as reaching out to one connection every one or two weeks. As you discuss your future with more and more trusted people in your circle, the conversations will energize you to do even more. Plus, you will be on more people's minds as opportunities arise.

Get Interview-Ready

Practice your interview skills to feel more confident. It's likely your toxic boss has eroded your confidence, so practice highlighting your work successes and accomplishments. Do you have a plan for how to explain why you're leaving your current position? Practice your interview skills with a trusted friend; doing so will be important if you have not interviewed in a long time.

When asked about why you're leaving, always explain your story in a positive light and do *not* say anything negative about your current boss, as that is a red flag for a potential employer, who may see your comments as disrespectful. There is no way for them to know the full story. Keep focused on the position and company in front of you, being curious and enthusiastic. Make your interview answers about seeking new challenges and opportunities for growth rather than trying to escape your toxic workplace. Employers like positivity and want to know you're applying for the right reasons, not just because it's an out from your current role.

The bottom line is that airing your dirty laundry is unprofessional, and an interview isn't the time or place to complain about your toxic boss, no matter how truly horrible they are. You have other outlets to do so, and starting any new job with healthy boundaries and learning to trust your new boss will be important, as we will discuss in Chapter 8: Thriving in Your Career Post–Toxic Boss.

FRAMING YOUR MOVE IN THE POSITIVE

Ajay sat across from the hiring manager, who asked him the dreaded question: Why was he leaving his current employer?

As tempting as it was to mention how incredibly toxic his boss was, he refrained and kept to the positive facts. He looked her in the eye and answered clearly, "I have learned a lot through my work at the brokerage, and have grown as a project manager and communicator. The variety of projects I managed exposed me to a lot of new areas and customer challenges. I'm now ready for my next opportunity to further grow by working in a different industry where my project management skills and experiences will bring value. I've heard great things about the growth opportunities at this bank and I think I'd be a solid fit with your learning culture."

Planned Happenstance

Planned happenstance is a career development concept that I first learned about in the early 2000s when I was exploring options for doing my PhD in psychology. Dr. John Krumboltz from Stanford was one of the professors who coined this term, and I got to meet with him a couple of times to discuss doing my doctoral studies with him. Ultimately, this opportunity wasn't meant to be—the program wasn't letting in new students during the timeframe I was applying—but the concept of *planned happenstance* is something I took away from our conversations that has helped many of my clients to successfully change jobs or careers.

Planned happenstance involves creating and seizing opportunities by intentionally putting yourself out there at unplanned, chance events. Unpredictable factors—like chance meetings, unlikely connections, unexpected job openings, or spur-of-the-moment conversations—often shape careers as much as careful planning does. Instead of seeing these events as purely random, planned happenstance encourages people to be open, adaptable, and proactive in recognizing and capitalizing on them.[1]

As you're looking for a new opportunity, are you putting yourself out there by meeting new people, attending events, and being open to conversations?

Here is how I utilize concepts from planned happenstance with my clients who are transitioning jobs and careers:

1. **Curiosity:** Remain curious about different career paths, including entrepreneurial paths and jobs or employers you may not have considered. These can lead to unexpected opportunities in your career.
2. **Persistence:** Be willing to pursue your goals even when obstacles arise or when the path forward is unclear. Exiting a toxic boss requires persistence, as your energy and confidence have been hit hard.
3. **Flexibility:** Be open to adapting to new opportunities and conversations as they come along. You never know where each will lead!
4. **Optimism:** Although it may be difficult, challenge yourself to see potential opportunities in any situation, including setbacks or detours in your job search.
5. **Risk-taking:** Take calculated risks, like attending a networking event that you normally wouldn't, joining a committee, or taking a course, to open doors to new career possibilities.

The path ahead is unpredictable, but chance will meet opportunity if you are open to it. You can leverage unexpected opportunities in ways that align with your strengths and interests and help facilitate a successful exit from your toxic boss.

Nontraditional Paths: Portfolio Careers and Entrepreneurship

Finding another job may not be your only option. More people are working contract jobs and doing entrepreneurial gigs than ever before. The *gig economy* is now a reality, where *multi-tracking* or holding down more than one work gig is common. This includes doing part-time roles, contracts, or being a freelancer for more than one organization. A *portfolio careerist* is another term for a person who streams their income from various sources rather than one full-time job.

Consider whether you are entrepreneurial in nature. Do you value a high level of control and autonomy over your work? Does the thought of starting, running, and growing your own business or venture excite you? For my part, I've always had an entrepreneurial spirit and my earlier toxic boss experiences propelled me into being a lifelong entrepreneur. But entrepreneurship isn't for everyone; it requires a tolerance for risk and ambiguity. Understanding the degree to which you're open to portfolio or entrepreneurial paths is an important part of self-insight in your career crossroad.

NAVIGATING A COMBINATION OF EMPLOYMENT WITH BUILDING A NEW BUSINESS

One of my research participants shared the following story of how she navigated combining entrepreneurship with part-time employment after taking a medical leave from her toxic boss:

Jessie, who worked in Human Resources in the tech industry, had reported to a Self-Serving Egomaniac and Narcissistic boss who was also a Control Freak. Jessie had strong grit and determination and the mindset that she could handle this, despite the increasing levels of abuse. But it caught up with her eventually—a panic attack came on when she was in her boss's office, resulting in her losing control of her body and slamming to the floor.

What happened next was what Jessie was hoping to avoid: She was compelled to take a stress leave.

She didn't realize how severe her physical symptoms had become until she went on leave. The silver lining was that this medical leave allowed her to start down a recovery path. Over time, she rebuilt her energy and confidence. Reviving her former entrepreneurial, creative business (which she had put a hold on after going back to full-time employment) was key to her.

In combination with her entrepreneurial venture, going back to a part-time position in the same company, this time under another leader, was necessary financially for Jessie, at least in the short term. But knowing she was rebuilding another path for herself helped her recover and grow.

Jessie's biggest takeaway was that you may need to leave, but sometimes you just can't, so it's important to focus on your recovery and growth in the interim.

Dr. Laura's Coaching Break: *Fueling your work search*

Ask yourself the following questions and write the answers in your journal:

1. What type of job am I looking for? Could now be the time to consider changing careers, or is a similar job under a better boss the way to go?
2. Is an internal move a possibility in my organization? Why or why not?
3. When it comes to external opportunities, am I leaning toward another full-time role or am I open to a portfolio or entrepreneurial path?
4. What times of the day or week will I be able to carve out chunks of time for job search activities?
5. Could I get up earlier to do my job search before my workday begins, or is it better to work on it in the evening after I've replenished myself with exercise, fresh air, and a healthy dinner? What about periodically taking a day off to complete this work?
6. Are my resume and cover letter updated? Do they reflect what I want to be doing next and the skills and experiences I want to take forward? Who can review each and give me feedback on improving them? (Note: A career counselor or job search advisor can be beneficial here.)
7. Is my online professional presence polished? (e.g., is my LinkedIn profile up to date and have I updated my connections?)
8. Whom in my network can I trust and who would be good to reach out to?

9. What are my goals for how many connections and conversations I will have each week/month?
10. Do I feel confident in my interview skills and have a plan for how to respond when asked why I want to leave my current position?

Creating your winning exit plan means setting a realistic and motivating timeline, focusing on your wellness plan to keep your battery charged, and preparing for and beginning your internal and/or external work search. Persistence and chance will come together in the form of *planned happenstance* to pave your ideal career path forward. Exiting a toxic boss is a reality that you *can* make come to fruition.

Takeaways from Chapter 4

- ✓ An exit plan is a strategy for how and on what timeline you will leave your current job and toxic boss.
- ✓ Creating an exit plan is a critical step toward regaining a sense of control and a healthier path forward in your career and life.
- ✓ Having an exit date that you write down and keep in mind—a *Good Riddance* (GR) date—will help you retake control of your career and life.
- ✓ As you are working on your exit plan, be sure to also create a personal wellness plan for nurturing your physical and mental health to keep your battery charged.

- ✓ Prepare for and set goals for your internal and/ or external work search, including updating your resume, cover letter, and LinkedIn profile, actively networking, and working on your interviewing skills.
- ✓ Put yourself out there to meet new people and forge new connections so that *planned happenstance* can play a role in landing your next (healthier) career opportunity.
- ✓ Stay open to exploring nontraditional paths, including portfolio careers and entrepreneurial options.

CHAPTER 5:

WHEN YOUR TOXIC BOSS DECIDES FOR YOU

"I didn't see it then, but it turned out that getting fired from Apple was the best thing that could have ever happened to me. The heaviness of being successful was replaced by the lightness of being a beginner again, less sure about everything. It freed me to enter one of the most creative periods of my life."

—Steve Jobs

Getting fired from Apple by its board of directors in 1985 must have been a terrible blow at the time, but as Steve Jobs later explained, it opened doors to evolving his career to new levels. He returned to Apple in 1997 to grow it into one of the world's most prolific brands. (As an aside: Steve Jobs was a difficult boss, there's no doubt about it. He was originally fired from Apple due to his confrontational management style and clashes with the board. Some may even argue he was toxic—specifically, a *Narcissist* and *Abusive A-Hole*. The point of this quote, though, is not to debate what type of boss he was but to shed light on the silver linings of being let go. A common thread through almost every client my team has encountered who has been laid off or fired is that, when they look back on it, they are grateful it happened. It forced them to look within themselves, realize how unhappy they were, and intentionally seek out something better.)

If you are still working for your toxic boss, it's important to be aware of the chance that you may be let go. If you are, this chapter will be critically important. It may also serve as a reminder that if you'd rather avoid your toxic boss deciding for you, you need to put your exit plan into action sooner rather than later (see Chapter 4: Creating a Winning Exit Plan).

Having the decision made for you is not easy at first; in fact, it can be incredibly emotionally difficult. When this happens, your ego gets massively bruised, and you may feel rejected by others in the organization who didn't intervene to save you from your toxic boss. You will go through many emotions, beginning with shock.

Céline got off the subway at her usual stop and automatically took the familiar path up and out into a Monday work morning at her law firm. The sky was gray, and she felt her anxiety build as she walked toward her office building. She had been reporting to her toxic boss, who was the most senior female partner in the firm, for fourteen months, and these had been the most difficult of her career. She was sure that this woman was a Sociopath and a Gaslighter; she deliberately hurt Céline's ability to succeed every chance she could and also twisted the truth so often that Céline found it almost impossible to remember the real facts. Most days at work, Céline felt like she was in a fog.

Céline had been a high-performing articling student at her last law firm before becoming an associate at this firm. When she started at this job, she'd first reported to another partner who was an excellent mentor and emphasized how he saw Céline as partner material—but then he'd retired and she'd been transferred to this toxic boss. Since then, her career had begun to unravel.

Céline's husband had been encouraging her to take a medical leave or quit; he promised he would support her through this transition. But Céline did not want to put that burden on him. She would rather find a job first, and then have the satisfaction of quitting. She was currently using what little energy she had left at the end of each workweek to put the finishing touches on her resume and LinkedIn profile.

Her heart beat faster as the elevator opened and she walked to her office. As she hung her coat, the HR director appeared at her doorway, startling her.

"Céline," she said, "we need to meet. Can you join us in the boardroom?"

Céline weakly responded, "Okay," and followed in a trance.

The meeting felt robotic and unreal. Her toxic boss was seated smugly on the other side of the table. The HR director sat down at her side, then gestured for Céline to sit across from them. The words "your role is no longer required" were spoken without emotion or appreciation for Céline's years of dedicated service at this company (four excellent years before the last fourteen months of hell reporting to this toxic boss).

As the meeting concluded, Céline was handed a manila envelope with a severance package tucked inside. The HR director ushered her out of the boardroom and let her know that her personal items would be couriered to her by

⇨

tomorrow. She was handed a taxi chit to get her home safely.

Céline caught a slight smile on her toxic boss's lips as she looked back one last time.

The HR director stuck to her side as she passed by her office to grab her coat, ensuring that she would leave the building quietly; she wasn't even afforded the opportunity to say goodbye to her dear colleagues.

As Céline's taxi wove through downtown and toward her house in the suburbs, she felt numb with shock. Where were the tears she expected? Why was she void of any emotion?

In a trancelike state, she texted her partner, "I've been let go." She was in another dimension as the taxi stopped at her condo building. Céline got out and walked up the path where she had started her Monday morning only an hour before.

The Shock Period

How your termination meeting goes will vary depending on the professionalism of your organization, your toxic boss, and whether HR is involved. In the context of remote work, being let go could be done virtually, which in some ways can be easier for the employee—this allows you to quickly exit the conversation without then finding yourself emotionally vulnerable in an office setting.

There are two main ways to have your employment terminated:

1. You can be "laid off," where you are told that your position is no longer needed and the decision is not tied to your performance.

2. You can be fired for "cause," which typically requires performance management conversations being documented leading up to the firing.

Firing for cause requires more work but typically saves a company from being required to give you a severance. It is not used nearly as often as laying off, which requires a severance package and puts the company at less risk of you fighting back legally. If you are on track to be fired, you will see that your boss is setting up for this through performance management discussions in the weeks and months leading up to being let go, as compared to a layoff, which can happen without any warning.

> *I went to a one-on-one meeting with my manager and HR virtually, on MS Teams. They told me that my contracted position was no longer available, as they'd finished the budget and were not going to have the full-time employee position that they thought they would for me. They proceeded to give me an ultimatum: take a severance package (which was way too low) or take a lower-level call center role with a pay cut. I took the call center role, as I felt I had no other option. But a week later, I saw a posting for a twelve-month contract for the exact same role I'd just held.*
>
> —LEARNING AND DEVELOPMENT ADVISOR, AVIATION INDUSTRY

Even if your toxic boss's terrible treatment of you is escalating and you know your role is in jeopardy, having your employment terminated will likely leave you shocked and stunned. It will feel so impersonal and happen so quickly that you won't have time to fully process what's going on until well after it's over.

Companies often say during a termination meeting that your position is "no longer required" or that you are "not a fit." Although you will likely be in shock, you may also feel a torrent of anger, hurt, and sadness that can be difficult to control. Tears may come immediately (or, if you're really in shock, they may not). Your heart will likely pound and your body may shake. These are all normal reactions to the feelings of shock and betrayal that a termination brings forth.

Although you can't control when a termination will take place, you *can* control how you react and carry yourself in the event that it does. Follow these tips during and directly following your termination to preserve your reputation and avoid giving your toxic boss further ammunition for why they believed they needed to let you go. Your reputation matters, as you never know when you will cross paths again with others from this organization, so burning a bridge is never a good idea.

What to Do During a Termination Meeting

1. Stay Calm and Remember to Breathe

Your nervous system will be on overdrive and your breathing will likely be shallow during this conversation. Try to breathe deeply, as even a couple of deep breaths can help you maintain a feeling of emotional control. Maintaining control is important during this difficult meeting; it will ensure that you won't say or do anything you'll later regret.

2. Don't Decide Anything Yet

It may be tempting to look at what they're offering in the moment, but it's not a good idea. You're not thinking clearly, and you need to review this package with a clear head and get advice if needed. Now is *not* the time to do that, and it's definitely not the time to sign anything, even if they pressure you to do so.

You may be threatened that if you don't sign now, you may not get the same good deal for severance. Don't believe it. This is *not* legal in North America and most Western countries, as you have a right to consult an employment lawyer regarding your package. Whether you decide to obtain legal advice or not, you still need the time to review under calmer circumstances and to discuss with loved ones. Take the time you need and deserve in order to get back to them with the decision that makes the most sense for you.

It is okay to ask any questions about next steps that you can think of on the spot, but you do not need to do so. Again, remember to reserve your right to follow up with more questions once you've reviewed the package provided.

Do *not* ask any questions about *why* you were terminated; now is not the time for that discussion, nor would they share their reasons even if you did ask (based on the advice of employment lawyers). All this will do is give your toxic boss a chance to inject some last-minute digs, so don't leave them the space for that!

3. Maintain Professionalism Through Your Shock

With the torrent of emotions raging like a river inside you, reacting strongly may be tempting. You may want to raise your voice, tell your boss off, or simply break down in tears. This is why you need to breathe deeply.

If your tears do flow, just ask for a tissue and exit as quickly as you can. There's no shame in crying; it's a normal and healthy human emotion and reaction to what has just happened.

If you run into anyone outside, don't vent or condemn your boss or organization, just politely say you need to go. Again, your reputation will follow you long after this horrible moment, so holding yourself professionally will serve you better in the future than will doing or saying something you may deeply regret.

What to Do After a Termination Meeting

1. Get Home Safely

Your employer may have arranged for transportation, but if they did not and you are feeling dazed or emotionally raw, you shouldn't drive. Instead, call a family member or friend to pick you up, take a taxi, do whatever is required to get you home safely.

2. Once You're Home, Let Your Emotions Flow

Emotional release is hard but necessary to process the grief, loss, hurt, and betrayal you will likely be feeling. Let your tears flow as long as they need to. Talk your feelings through with a loved one; even if you're feeling ashamed or embarrassed, it is worth sharing your news with someone trusted so they can support and comfort you. You may also try journaling or screaming in the quiet of your home . . . whatever ways you need to release your emotions, they must come out in order to heal from this traumatic event (yes, working for and being let go by a toxic boss is a form of trauma).

3. Be Kind to Yourself

Know that this is happening as it should and there will be much healthier opportunities ahead for you and your career. Nurture yourself in whatever small and healthy ways you can (e.g., a hot bubble bath, a cup of tea, a walk).

4. Take Some Time to Process

As tempting as it may be to jump into a document/package review so you can decide on next steps, give yourself a bit of time first to process what just happened. Try not to fall for any false sense of urgency created by your employer (i.e., a deadline to respond/accept the package offer). Remember, their urgency needn't be yours. Do not make any rash financial decisions, as your logical brain won't be fully on while your emotional one is in overdrive.

5. Avoid the Temptation to Numb

Alcohol and drugs may make you feel better temporarily, but they will also leave you vulnerable to high anxiety, depressed feelings, and a poor sleep afterward—all of which will leave you less able to process your emotions or think logically through your financial decisions, severance package review, and next steps. You want your brain firing the best it can as you navigate your next steps in your career journey after being let go by your toxic boss, so take care of yourself.

Céline felt numb until she talked to her partner on her cell phone while curled up on the sofa. When he expressed deep empathy, she shed a waterfall of tears. When she hung up from the call she continued crying, her body trembling with the emotions of not only that morning's termination but also all the toxic behaviors her boss had subjected her to leading up to this: the subtle attacks on her intelligence, the constant questioning about why Céline did things the way she did despite having clearly requested earlier that they be done that way. For months, Céline had walked on eggshells each day, wondering how her boss was going to throw her under the bus next, and the resulting mental confusion and self-doubt that plagued her had made her feel like she was losing the sharp thinking abilities she'd always prided herself on.

Making her way to the bathroom, Céline ended up on the floor, sobbing uncontrollably. Once she had no more tears to shed, rage crept in. How F-ing unfair this all was. She looked at her swollen face in the mirror and screamed at the top of her lungs. The wrongness of all this filled her with rage, making her heart pound and her fists clench. Her emotions were intense and raw, and she wondered if she'd ever feel normal again.

Working Through an Emotional Hurricane

As was the case with Céline, as your shock wears off, or even alongside that shock, a range of different emotions may begin to unleash themselves.

Each of us is unique, and the way we experience and process emotions happens in different ways in our minds and bodies. You may quickly cycle through various emotions, feeling an unpredictable hurricane of feelings around what has transpired. This is a normal period to experience and you need to go through it to get beyond it, like moving through a storm to see the sunlight on the other side.

Here are some common emotions you may experience in the aftermath of being let go by a toxic boss:

Anger

You may feel intense anger at the unfairness of the situation—especially if you were a strong performer and if you tried to raise the alarm bells internally (e.g., to Human Resources), which went unaddressed. If this betrayal and these feelings of mistreatment fill you with rage, your anger may bring about the following:

- Wanting to scream or physically let it out
- Your body feeling extremely tense
- Elevated heart rate and blood pressure
- Persistent thoughts of wanting your toxic boss to suffer as they've made you suffer

All of these are normal reactions to what you're going through, but you need to manage them in healthy ways (I'll share more about how to do this at the end of this list of emotions).

Sadness

You may also experience waves of sadness due to the feelings of betrayal and loss of your position. If you liked your work and organization prior to reporting to your toxic boss, you are especially likely to go through a period of grieving this loss. Sadness is a normal emotion; instead of bottling it up, let it flow through and out of your mind. Any or all of the following can be great ways to let out your feelings:

- Tears
- Conversations with loved ones and friends
- Journaling
- Therapy/counseling

Doubt/Confusion

Feelings of doubt and confusion are also common during this timeframe. You may find yourself ruminating about what you could have done differently and wanting to understand how things turned out this way. It's normal to struggle with a need to make sense of it all, as you haven't gotten proper closure from your organization. Talking it through with others, particularly those who have been let go from the same organization or boss, may help. Learning to acknowledge to yourself that you may never understand what happened will come in time.

Guilt/Regret

You may feel a sense of guilt that you contributed to this outcome or that you could have done things differently to avoid being let go. As your mind flashes back to your toxic-boss journey, you may regret things you did or didn't do, or even that you didn't quit prior to being released by them. These feelings are normal but cause unnecessary pain and should be released as you move forward. You can't change or control the past, and must focus on the present as you recover.

Anxiety

Feelings of anxiety include persistent worry or fear. You may worry about finding another opportunity or whether justice will prevail if you decide to take legal action against your former employer. (Reminder: We discussed the factors that go into whether to take legal action in Chapter 3, and doing so requires a careful weighing of the pros and cons.) It's normal to worry and ruminate about which way to go when it comes to taking legal action, as doing so is a major decision and can entail serious financial and emotional cost.

In addition to its emotional effects, anxiety often has physical impacts, such as:

- Increased heart rate
- Rapid breathing
- Excessive sweating
- Trembling
- Stomach upset

When it comes to your brain, you may have racing or looping thoughts; it's common to find yourself overthinking everything, having difficulty concentrating, and catastrophizing the worst possible outcome (e.g., *I'll never be able to get a job and I'll end up homeless*). Anxiety also impacts sleep, causing you to have insomnia and nighttime awakenings.

Strategies for Processing and Releasing Your Emotions

Although the emotional hurricane you are facing may feel uncontrollable, there are things you can do to help ease the intensity, process what you are feeling, and find greater calm amidst this storm. These include:

- **Physical activity:** A brisk walk or run, safely using a punching bag, or whatever form of physical exercise works for you.
- **Screaming in a private space:** Say what you would love to say to your toxic boss and those who enabled them. Yell with all your energy to release your anger, like Céline did in the story you read earlier in this chapter.
- **Journaling your angry thoughts:** Writing, ideally pen-to-paper, is a great way to process and release a variety of emotions.
- **Remembering how awesome you are:** You are now at a low point. Summon *past you*, the one who was riding high in their career, and channel them back into your mind. Go back to your timeline to review and build on it. Tell yourself the story again, as you would to a friend (maybe a few days after the event,

once you've taken a bit of time to just *be*). This will help reframe negative thoughts about yourself, remembering that this was not about *you* but about your toxic *boss's* cruel behavior.

- **Expressing your feelings to a therapist:** Talk through your anger and how it makes you feel and think. Having an honest dialogue and learning some immediate coping mechanisms is highly recommended. (We'll explore types of therapy in greater detail in Chapter 6: Recovering from a Toxic Boss.)
- **Mindfulness/meditation:** Grounding yourself through intentional breathing and meditation may seem difficult to do, but starting gradually, with even a few deep breaths or a five-minute calming meditation, can make a difference in feeling more grounded. There are many good apps for this purpose, including Insight Timer and Calm, that can provide specific meditations for calming emotions like anxiety, fear, and anger. There are also freely available meditations on platforms like YouTube.

Determining Your Next Steps

In most cases, you will be given a severance package with your termination, unless you were fired or terminated with *cause*, as described earlier. In that case, formal *performance management* should have occurred. If this didn't occur, yet you were fired with cause and no severance, you should consider speaking to an employment lawyer about your rights and what you may be entitled to.

> *I was offered a poor package. I had to fight and spend over $5,000 to simply get what was fair.*
>
> —MANAGER AT A NONPROFIT ORGANIZATION

Reviewing your severance package carefully is important, and looking up the severance rules in your jurisdiction to ensure your employer is at least meeting their legal requirements is recommended. You will of course also want to revisit your employment contract to see what might have been stated regarding severance. Important considerations include whether they are offering the minimum amount of severance (i.e., number of months or years of pay) based on the number of years worked, and how long your benefits will continue. But nothing beats talking to an employment lawyer who understands the nuances of these documents, as there's the letter of the law but there are also considerations that may lead to more months of severance being appropriate.

> *Make sure to really listen to your partner, family, and lawyer regarding the fairness of your package. I've noticed that, at this stage, people are so spent and have no fight left in them, so accept much less than they should just to get this over with.*
>
> *You may feel instant relief just accepting a package now, thinking you'll quickly find something else—but what if you don't find something else right away? My advice is to be careful not to subsidize your toxic boss's bad behavior with your stress and/or your family's financial security.*
>
> —LAWYER AND FORMER DIRECTOR AT A POST-SECONDARY INSTITUTION

Legal Action: The Pros and Cons

As we discussed in Chapter 3, taking legal action is a choice to consider that has both pros and cons. (If you want to refresh your memory, refer to *Option 4: Take Legal Action* in the *So, What Are Your Options?* section of Chapter 3.) Now that your employment has been terminated, how your severance was handled adds an additional layer to your situation.

Following is advice from one of my research participants who is a lawyer and was a director at a post-secondary institute. She experienced a toxic boss who she describes as a *Dishonest Manipulator*, *Great Divider*, and *Gaslighter*. She has firsthand experience with taking legal action against this toxic boss. Keep in mind, the decision to pursue legal action or not is extremely subjective. To help you make this decision, think long and hard about why you would be doing so. I've summarized my research participant's key recommendations for what you should consider before taking legal action:

- Is it purely financial?
- Are you motivated to right a wrong or correct an injustice?
- Do you want to set an example for your child/friend/sibling?
- Does your toxic boss remind you of a bully you dealt with in the past who you simply cannot allow to get away with it "this" time?

Your *why(s)* around pursuing legal action will be unique to your situation, and there's no hard-and-fast rule about whether it will make sense based on the reasons listed. These are meant to guide your thinking as to whether legal action is a path that makes sense for you, your loved ones, and your career.

Regardless of how it goes, you will have no control over how others (and your employer) will react to your filing. Understanding your *whys*, or motivations, will go a long way toward helping you through the inevitable lows or doubts that will come if you pursue this path.

This participant also had this to say about standing up for herself, which may or may not apply to your situation: *In my case, I had dealt with a toxic boss before and not stood up for myself. I then went on to do precisely the kind of work that made me understand the issue better. I'd learned a great deal about complaint/legal options and told myself that if I ever faced a situation like this again and my informal attempts failed that I would file an official complaint. So, I did not think that I would be okay walking away; I knew I'd regret it. I would feel like I had not learned my lesson, that I'd let myself down. Because of this, pursuing legal action was right for me.*

Dr. Laura's Coaching Break: *Identifying your legal action support team*

If you choose to pursue legal avenues, you will need lots of support, as it can be an emotionally turbulent journey. Think about the kind of support you have access to and will need. This support falls into two categories: professional and personal.

Who will you need to recruit to your team? Note in your journal the people that fall under each category:

- Professionals: a lawyer, a therapist, a doctor, other care providers, childcare, etc.

- Personal: spouse/partner, friends, parents, children, pets, siblings, gym buddy, etc.

Next, answer the following questions in your journal:

1. What will everyone's role be and who will you go to for what? Be prepared to make this clear (e.g., letting your family know that you need to limit conversations about legal strategy to your lawyer for your own mental health, but that you welcome questions and support around your emotional state).
2. If you're in a relationship, pay special attention to your spouse/significant other and the state of your relationship. Can your relationship handle this extra stress at this time? Is your spouse supportive and in the right headspace to walk this road with you? Do they want or need this for you (and for them)?
3. What financial resources can you devote to pursuing legal action? How much will you spend, and when will you know you've hit your limit? Will you set an amount at which you'll walk away, regardless of outcome, or will you take this the whole way no matter what?
4. How much time do you expect this to take? (Hint: It will probably be much longer than you think).
5. Will there be lasting impacts on your career? How might this affect your ability to find other work? Could there be potential consequences for your reputation in your field and in your market?

Know that there is absolutely no shame in just walking away and living to fight another day, if that is what's best for you and your family and your mental health. You do not have a responsibility to right the wrongs of your workplace or fight on others' behalf. Do what is right for you.

If you *do* take legal action against your employer, be prepared to lose the support of colleagues and work friends. The gates of the company/institution will also slam shut if you take legal action or sue. People who you expect to be there for you may let you down, and when that happens it will hurt. But others who you may not have expected to may rise to the occasion and show up in lovely ways. Be ready to find out who your real friends are!

When your boss decides for you and terminates your employment, either legally or illegally, you will experience a myriad of emotions. Ultimately, you're being set free from a toxic scenario and there will be better opportunities ahead. To get through this difficult period, you will need to work through your emotions and manage your reactions and next steps ahead. Hopefully, doing so will help you feel clearer and more able to deal with the financial and legal decisions ahead—while simultaneously preserving your well-being and dignity.

Takeaways from Chapter 5

- ✓ Being let go by a toxic boss is incredibly difficult, so knowing what you *can* control throughout the process will help you come out the other end more successfully.
- ✓ Although there may be signs of a termination coming, most people go through an initial period of feeling shocked and stunned.

- ✓ During the termination meeting, stay calm, maintain professionalism, and don't sign anything that day.
- ✓ Following termination, you'll likely be catapulted into an emotional hurricane (including anger, sadness, doubt, confusion, and anxiety), so take care of yourself, take time to process, and get the right emotional supports in place.
- ✓ There are key strategies to process and release your emotions, including being physically active, journaling, working with a therapist (including somatic therapies), and practicing mindfulness/ meditation, to name a few.
- ✓ If you were terminated *without cause*, determine whether your severance package is sufficient. Consult legal advice if needed to understand if you're eligible for more.
- ✓ If you were fired (or terminated) with cause, and performance management didn't occur, you may have a legal case. But pursuing legal action has pros and cons, and understanding these is important as you make this decision.
- ✓ If you do decide to pursue legal action, identify who should be a part of your legal action support team and what role(s) each person should play on that team.

Part 3: Life Beyond a Toxic Boss

"Don't let yesterday take up too much of today."
—Will Rogers

PART 3 INTRODUCTION:

THE GRASS IS GREENER

Part 2 of this book helped you explore your options around leaving your toxic boss. Crafting and executing an exit plan hopefully led you to leave your toxic boss, whether to another role or to another organization. Or, perhaps you had enough and decided to quit, or your toxic boss decided for you. Whatever transpired, here you are on the other side of a toxic relationship, with the opportunity to recover and enjoy a much healthier work future where the grass *is* greener.

The following chapters will help you feel empowered to proactively manage your career journey moving forward. Chapter 6 will explore the aftereffects of having reported to a toxic boss, and the proven methods of self-care and healing that can help you emerge stronger than before. Many of these self-care methods have come from my research participants who have gotten away from a toxic boss and are now back in control of their lives and careers, as well as evidence-based recommendations from my field of psychology. You will feel empowered to recover any damage your toxic boss has done, knowing you have the ability and tools to fully recover.

Chapter 7 will focus on how you can avoid ever working for a toxic boss again by learning to identify the warning signs during the recruitment and hiring process. You will be armed with tools and techniques for investigating whether a workplace is healthy or toxic, thereby minimizing your chances of working for another toxic boss.

Chapter 8 empowers you to thrive in your career post–toxic boss. You will learn how to rebuild your confidence, take charge of your own career, and build trust with your next boss. The concept of empowering "You, Inc." will help you take charge as the CEO of your own career. You will learn tips and strategies for how to proactively manage your career journey going forward. You'll learn about your personal trust meter and make a plan to get off on the best foot possible. You'll hear success stories from other toxic boss survivors. You'll finish this chapter feeling energized about navigating your career path post–toxic boss, and inspired by the knowledge that the grass really is greener on the other side.

CHAPTER 6:

RECOVERING FROM A TOXIC BOSS

> *"I survived because the fire inside me burned brighter than the fire around me."*
>
> —JOSHUA GRAHAM

Recovering from a toxic boss is a healing process that takes time, support, and lots of self-care. Regardless of whether you move quickly on to another job or have a period of time off, your recovery and healing process will need attention. Many experiences under a toxic boss—being manipulated, bullied, harassed, gaslit, or controlled—are forms of trauma.

Each of the toxic boss personas and behaviors we covered in Chapter 2 impacts your well-being. However, if you've determined that your boss is one of the bolded personas on the next page, you're more likely to have experienced trauma and may need more recovery time to heal from your experience:

- Self-Serving Egomaniac
- Control Freak
- Great Divider
- **Dishonest Manipulator**
- **The Unethical Corrupter**
- **Abusive A-Hole**
- **Narcissist or Sociopath**
- **Gaslighter**

If you've worked under one of these five **bolded** personas, your self-confidence will more likely have been eroded, and recovering from this will require much self-care and self-love. Working for a toxic boss can somewhat mirror the experience of a victim involved in an abusive romantic relationship. Specifically, a toxic boss and an abusive partner can exhibit similar behaviors because both dynamics involve imbalances of power, manipulation, and emotional strain.

A toxic boss can be hard to escape due to the financial and career impacts of quitting. For example, your job likely provides a steady income and benefits, contributes to your career identity, and perhaps even constitutes your primary social network. These factors create a level of dependency, making it difficult to make a clean break, similar to certain factors that tie a person to a toxic romantic relationship.

Take a moment to go back to the toxic boss personas that you identified in the Chapter 2 checklist titled *What personas best describe your toxic boss?* If your boss qualified as any of these five most harmful personas, it will be extra important for you to get professional support from a therapist (see the *Your Recovery Buffet* section of this chapter for more on this).

Upon leaving my job, I believe I had post-traumatic stress disorder (PTSD). This condition was verified by several others who left the company and had the same issue. Honestly, it took several months for the anxious feelings and ruminating on this experience to go away, but every day I was so very thankful for leaving the organization, as I knew the day I left that my healing would begin.

—EXECUTIVE AT AN INVESTMENT COMPANY

The impact of working for a toxic boss is shocking and it takes a long time to recover from. I think of myself as a very resilient person, so acknowledging that I just couldn't do it any longer was like admitting defeat—like somehow my toxic boss had "won" or was somehow stronger. It took me a long time to recover emotionally, mentally, and physically and reframe what had happened—that the situation was a reflection of her, not me.

—VP AT AN ENERGY COMPANY

It took a year to shake the negativity off.

—FINANCIAL SERVICES/INVESTMENT ADVISOR ON WALL STREET

If You Have PTSD from Your Toxic Boss

According to the *Diagnostic and Statistical Manual of Mental Disorders (DSM-5-TR)*, post-traumatic stress disorder (PTSD) is a mental health condition triggered by experiencing or witnessing a traumatic event.[1] The traumatic events people typically refer to when they talk about PTSD are life-threatening events like war, terrorist acts, serious injury, or sexual violence.

Working with a toxic boss is not typically life-threatening in the physical sense, but it can still cause PTSD. This experience can lead you to feel, for example, that your career is over and you're going to end up unemployable and destitute. I've heard and seen this extreme thinking/catastrophizing in my own clients and through the experiences shared by research participants.

The symptoms of PTSD include:

- Intrusive flashbacks and nightmares that cause intense distress and persistent negative beliefs about yourself or the world
- Impairment to your daily functioning, like difficulty concentrating

These symptoms can make you feel like you're losing your mind and are incredibly difficult and anxiety-provoking. If you have these types of specific symptoms post–toxic boss for more than a month, and to an extent that your ability to function in your daily life is significantly impaired, it will be important to get professional help. Included in this chapter is a list of different trauma therapies for you to consider. PTSD is a more extreme result of working under toxic leadership, but whatever your experiences have been, there is plenty in this chapter to help with your specific recovery.

> *I experienced nightmares for a year after I left. My mind would bring up episodes with my former toxic boss, but I tried not to dwell on it.*
>
> —COLLEGE DIRECTOR AND FACULTY MEMBER

Recovering from a Toxic Boss Takes Time

Shiva wondered if she would ever feel like herself again. It had been a month since she'd quit working for her toxic boss at a marketing firm, and she continued to be plagued by anxiety and self-doubt. Her thoughts were like flies buzzing around her head; when she tried to swat them away, they would quickly come back. Thoughts like, "Look what you've done, you quit before having another job. Now it will be impossible to get hired! You should have just sucked it up. You're weak and useless." Or, "If you had just worked harder, you could have impressed your boss and made things easier. Now you're the one suffering and they're still happily employed."

These nasty thoughts were getting Shiva down, depleting her energy so she wasn't working out or getting outdoors. Also, she wasn't making much progress on her job search; instead, she was staying in her pajamas all day, scrolling through social media, wishing she had someone else's life.

Shiva's stuck in a negative headspace, feeling lethargic and low-energy. The constant negative voice in her head is making her situation worse. Her situation represents a vicious cycle in that her low mood and lack of energy prevent her from doing things to build energy, therefore further depleting her. In this state, she will make little progress on the job-search front and is at risk of falling into a depression.

This is why it's important to be aware of *your* emotional and physical symptoms, and to make an action plan for your toxic-boss recovery journey as soon as possible. If you're feeling depressed and unmotivated after several weeks, you'll definitely want to ensure you're getting professional support to aid your recovery.

Many research study participants shared that they had to learn to be patient and give themselves time to recover. Many still thought of themselves as recovering months, or even a couple of years, later. It took longer than they expected to shake off the negativity and feelings of inadequacy they were left with post–toxic boss. The more emotional and physical symptoms you've accumulated while working for a toxic boss, the longer your recovery may take. In the next section of this chapter, you will complete a checklist that will help you better understand your current symptoms as you navigate the best recovery tools.

When it comes to your recovery, it's normal to have a difficult time initially, but you should gradually start feeling better in the weeks and couple of months that follow this initial slump. Some of my research participants needed several months of not working to recover, while others were back in a new role and able to recover while working in a healthier environment.

> *Recovery did not feel very hard because I'm very fortunate to have found a new position with such understanding bosses. They instilled trust and autonomy, which I thought I would never be able to gain because I was so micromanaged before.*
>
> —LEGAL ASSISTANT

We will now look at your symptoms to help you better understand these, and in turn what options from my *Recovery Buffe*t may best support your recovery process.

Dr. Laura's Coaching Break: *Your symptoms post–toxic boss*

So now that you're on the other side of your toxic boss, how are you feeling and doing on a daily basis? Let's explore the types of psychological and physical pain that toxic bosses can leave you with. Some of these may be similar to those you were experiencing *while* working for your toxic boss (see checklist in Chapter 1), and some may be new. How each person is impacted by a toxic boss varies widely, so understanding the impacts you're personally experiencing is a first step toward addressing and healing from these.

The emotional, physical, and behavioral impacts listed on the following pages have come from my research participants as well as my experience in the field of psychology. The total of your scores here will give you a means to gauge the degree of symptoms you are dealing with and inform the types of recovery options you will need.

Place a checkmark beside those that you are currently experiencing and write in your journal additional ways that each area has impacted you:

1. DEPRESSION

- ❑ I am feeling very sad, unhappy, or low
- ❑ I have a negative voice in my head that says things will never get better
- ❑ I am crying regularly about what I went through with my toxic boss
- ❑ I no longer enjoy or look forward to the things I used to

Total items selected: ______ /4

Additional comments about my depression/sadness caused by my toxic boss (note these in your journal)

Note: There are free depression screening tools online, such as this one from Mental Health America—https://screening.mhanational.org/screening-tools/depression—but if you have felt depressed for more than two weeks, it's imperative that you connect with your family doctor and a licensed therapist to more accurately assess your depressive symptoms and form a treatment plan.

Shiva continued to spiral for many weeks, and feelings of hopelessness took over. She could no longer find any joy in her life and dreaded waking up to face another sad day. Depression had set in. As she was living alone, she was able to keep her mental state hidden for a long time—until, finally, her best friend insisted on coming by.

Shiva could not stop crying during her friend's visit, and upon their insistence, she agreed to book in with her family doctor as well as a local therapist. Now, when she looks back on these dark days, she credits her best friend with being the push she needed to get help. Through a *combination of therapy and an antidepressant*, Shiva was able to once again work out and have energy to put into her job search.*

***Note** that there are non-pharmaceutical remedies that can help with depressive symptoms, which you could explore with a naturopathic doctor. There is also healing power in meditation, mindfulness, and exercise. Medication is a personal choice, and I recommend exploring your options with trusted professionals to figure out what works for you.

2. BURNOUT

- ❑ I am feeling exhausted and depleted of energy
- ❑ I feel removed or distant from my career, like it no longer matters
- ❑ I have negative or cynical thoughts about working
- ❑ I feel like I can no longer do a good job
- ❑ I no longer believe I have what it takes to succeed in my career

Total items selected: ______ /5

Additional comments about my burnout caused by my toxic boss (note these in your journal)

3. ANXIETY

- ❑ I am constantly worried when it comes to my future
- ❑ I often ruminate about what happened with my toxic boss
- ❑ I am scared about potentially reporting to another toxic boss

- ❑ I feel paranoid that my toxic boss will find a way to harm my career going forward (e.g., spread things about me that will put my reputation at risk)

Total items selected: ______ /4

Additional comments about my anxiety caused by my toxic boss (note these in your journal)

4. PHYSICAL SYMPTOMS

- ❑ I'm experiencing muscle pain or tension that I did not have prior to my toxic boss experience (e.g., back pain, jaw pain/clenching)
- ❑ I'm experiencing stomach or gut issues
- ❑ I'm experiencing headaches or migraines
- ❑ My blood pressure is elevated

Total items selected: ______ /4

Additional comments about my physical symptoms caused by my toxic boss (note these in your journal)

5. BEHAVIORAL CHANGES

- ❑ I'm having difficulty either falling and/or staying asleep
- ❑ I have nightmares about my toxic boss
- ❑ My eating habits are unhealthy (e.g., eating too much or too little, eating more junk food)
- ❑ I'm drinking more alcohol and/or using more drugs than before
- ❑ My self-care has suffered (e.g., I'm no longer exercising or taking time for my wellness)

- ❑ I'm binge-watching shows or online content to escape from my situation

Total items selected: ______ /6

Additional comments about my behavioral changes caused by my toxic boss (note these in your journal)

6. PERSONAL LIFE/RELATIONSHIP STRAIN

- ❑ What I've been through with my toxic boss has impacted my personal life (e.g., my relationship with my spouse or partner is strained)
- ❑ My partner/family has been expressing frustration that I'm not myself (e.g., I'm short-fused or unhappy) even though I no longer work for the toxic boss

Total items selected: ______ /2

Additional comments about my personal life/relationship strain caused by my toxic boss (note these in your journal)

7. OTHER IMPACTS

- ❑ I regularly feel angry about what I went through
- ❑ My ability to focus and process information has been impacted (e.g., brain fog, hard time learning new things, blanking out)
- ❑ My memory has been impacted (e.g., vocabulary/name recall, remembering important deadlines or information)

Total items selected: ______ /3

Additional comments and other impacts from your toxic boss not previously mentioned (note these in your journal)

Now add up your scores across all items to get your total out of 28.

Total Score: ______ /28

If you scored **20 or more**—You are facing a **STORM of impacts,** and need to get help immediately. Your health is at risk, and it's imperative that you speak with your doctor, a therapist, and other practitioners that can help you in your healing journey.

If you scored **14 or more**—You are facing a **HEIGHTENED number of impacts**, and need to put a recovery plan in place, which may involve various practitioners as well as self-care. If you selected any of the items in the depression category, it's critical that you get professional help.

If you scored **7 or more**—You are facing a **MODERATE number of impacts**, and it's important to put in place your recovery plan. The type of items selected will determine the nature of the recovery interventions needed. If you selected any of the items in the depression category, it's critical that you get professional help.

If you scored **6 or fewer**—You are doing well, as you are suffering a relatively lower number of impacts, but you still have **SOME impacts** to address. Unless your score was zero, it's still important to create a recovery plan focused on these impacts. Even a single impact should be addressed in a recovery plan as part of your toxic-boss healing journey.

Now that you've completed this checklist, how are you feeling about where you're at post–toxic boss? You may be feeling overwhelmed if you checked off a lot of items and are at the STORM or HEIGHTENED impact levels. Has this exercise helped validate just how much your toxic boss experience has affected you?

Know that these emotional and physical impacts are common for people who worked for a toxic boss, but you *can* recover and feel like your amazing self again! I have seen firsthand with my research participants and clients how transformed they feel once they recover from a toxic boss. The good news is, there are plenty of recovery options, and you can choose what will work best for you.

Your Recovery Buffet

Think of your *Recovery Buffet* as a range of healing options, choosing what best fits your individual requirements. But know that a combination of methods will give you more forms of support and a greater likelihood of addressing your physical, mental, emotional, and spiritual healing needs. Just like at a buffet restaurant, you don't have to try just one item; think about trying a healthy mix of items to fill your toxic-boss recovery appetite. If you like an item, go back for more. If it isn't working for you, you don't have to finish it. Recovery is about trying and choosing the best mix of items for your unique healing journey.

The following recovery options are organized into different categories and are meant to be used in combination with one another. As you're reviewing these, think about which you'll try as part of your toxic-boss recovery journey. Remember that the effort and energy you put into your recovery equals the healing benefits you experience.

Buffet Starters—Self-Care Practices

These "starters" include a variety of self-care practices that are relatively quick and free or inexpensive to do. Many of these have worked for my research participants and clients, but not all of them may suit your individual needs and preferences. Consider which of them may be worth incorporating into your own toxic-boss healing journey:

1. Rest

Taking the time to rest is a fundamental part of recovery, especially when you're burned out and healing from trauma. If you're working another job already, be sure to schedule fewer activities outside of work so you can take some necessary downtime. Or perhaps you can arrange to work a reduced workweek for a period of time.

> *Working fewer days gave me time to recover, eat healthier, be more physically active, and get into a healthier routine.*
>
> —CONSULTANT

> *I needed a period of time to deeply rest in order to let go.*
>
> —FORMER DIRECTOR OF A NONPROFIT ORGANIZATION

2. Re-Engage in Activities You Enjoy

Focus on things you enjoy doing, such as reconnecting with hobbies and activities you didn't do while working for your toxic boss. Many people end up dropping activities they enjoy as their work becomes all-consuming under a toxic boss. Go back to doing things you love.

3. Go Traveling

Get yourself to another destination for a change of scenery and a chance to rejuvenate. This doesn't have to mean flying somewhere; it could simply mean driving to the mountains, a body of water, or a nearby retreat, or going to stay with friends or family.

4. Eat Healthy

Take the time to prepare and cook healthy meals. Avoid alcohol, caffeine, and high-sodium and high-sugar foods as much as possible during your recovery.

5. Take Time in Nature

This may include walking, hiking, camping, skiing, etc., depending on what you enjoy most. Check out my podcast episode on the power of nature for work–life wellness, included in the Resources section at the back of the book, for some ideas on how to implement this powerful strategy.

6. Spend Time with a Pet

Time with an animal can help your healing; they can serve as wonderful emotional supports, and they can encourage you to exercise more.

> *I adopted a dog, which was great therapy for healing from my toxic boss. I walked over 14,000 steps a day as a result.*
>
> —DIRECTOR IN HEALTHCARE

7. Exercise

Daily physical activity is a key part of recovery and good mental and emotional health. This does not require an intense workout every day, but rather figuring out how you will keep active on a daily and weekly basis. Your body needs time to heal between intense workouts, so try to vary your more challenging days with easier days. A combination of cardio, strength, and mobility (e.g., stretching/yoga) is recommended. Walking as many days as possible is also an excellent habit on your healing journey and beyond. There's something special about the combination of exercising *and* being outdoors, as it exposes us to nature and its healing powers, and creates more positive feelings through releasing endorphins, even if all you do is walk briskly. Other outdoor exercise options include hiking, skiing, snowshoeing, skating, rollerblading, tennis, pickle ball, tai chi, and outdoor bootcamps, to name a few.

Philip felt emotionally and physically drained from working under a Dishonest Manipulator, Narcissist, and Sociopath boss for the past year. He lived near a park that he found peaceful, and had in fact bought his condo because it overlooked the green space. Yet he hadn't walked there in months. He'd been working sixty-hour weeks, and even though he'd been working from home three days each week, on those days he worked even longer hours than when at the office.

The morning after his employment was terminated, Philip lay in bed ruminating about how terribly unfair this all was. He had always been a star performer, and the way one toxic boss could unravel that in only twelve months was beyond him. His jaw clenched and his chest tightened as angry and resentful thoughts churned in his head.

When Philip finally rolled out of bed, he decided to open his blinds, and there stood the beautiful park. He knew then what he must do . . . go for a walk.

As he walked the winding paths among the trees and flowers, he breathed deeply. He sat on a bench and contemplated the last year and what his future might look like. He took in the sounds of the birds and noticed the children's laughter on the playground. He noted the reflection of green in the pond, and the ripples in the shimmering water.

Life would go on, and his career would move forward in a healthier way; this was clear to him now. Walking and thinking led him to a much calmer headspace, and from that day forward, walking that park would be his daily habit during his recovery journey and beyond.

8. Connection and Emotional Support

Connecting with others is a powerful part of healing from a toxic boss. Friends and loved ones who care about you can listen and provide validation and support, making a real difference. Not all your friends and family will be good listeners, or be patient or empathetic with your healing journey, so select carefully whom you will open up to about your toxic boss healing journey. But open up to someone. Even if you have only one or two close supporters, they will be a gift in your recovery and will appreciate the chance to support you, as you would do the same for them. In addition to sharing your journey with a few key supporters in your life, connecting with others who have also survived a toxic boss, or even have worked for the same boss as you did, can be healing as well. Those who have been through similar experiences can deeply understand and empathize, and show you that you're not alone.

9. Mindfulness/Meditation

Touched upon throughout this book, mindfulness and meditation are powerful practices while you're working for a toxic boss, during your recovery, and as an ongoing wellness practice. Mindfulness involves taking time to focus on the present and is often done through intentional, deep breathing exercises. Meditation is a form of mindfulness, allowing you to focus on the present, slow down your racing thoughts, and set affirmations and intentions. Research has found that even brief mindfulness meditation practices benefit our well-being, regardless of the specific meditation type. Fundamentally, no differences were found between the effects of short and long sitting/movement meditations.[2]

I started a meditation practice in 2020, when I was invited to a "21 Days of Abundance" group by a friend on WhatsApp.

Committing to twenty-one days in a row allowed me to truly experience the grounding and manifestation powers of meditation, and by the end of those three weeks I was hooked. Now I do at least ten to fifteen minutes of meditation first thing in the morning almost every day. It helps me be more intentional, calm, grounded, and productive throughout my day.

There are many great apps designed to help with this practice; Insight Timer, Presence, and Calm are a few that I use and recommend to my clients. These apps have specific meditations for calming emotions like anxiety, fear, and anger. You can search within each app for your specific challenge or purpose, such as calming anxiety, healing, or manifesting success, to find the meditations you need.

10. Journaling

The "Dr. Laura's Coaching Breaks" I've included throughout this book incorporate journaling for a reason: it's a powerful healing and development tool on so many levels.

First, it's a method to gain deeper self-insight. Putting pen to paper, or even typing out your thoughts, can help you understand the impacts your toxic boss has had on you, and to make sense of these experiences.

Second, journaling is a great way to process and release the many emotions you will experience as you go through your healing journey. Some days will be harder than others, and your journal will be an outlet for writing about your ups and downs, as well as setting intentions for how you want to experience each new day. I like to set three intentions each day for how I will "be" or come across throughout the day, such as to be loving, show appreciation, or practice patience. (Note: I've made the mistake of letting my journal become a to-do list of goals and action items before, but this is not its ideal purpose.

Creating a task list is too detailed and replicates what should be in your planning system or agenda. Your intentions are bigger and broader than tasks or to-dos, and help you to manifest how you want to move forward in your journey.)

Third, a daily gratitude practice is a powerful way to build joy and optimism back into your work and life, post–toxic boss. Gratitude practices involve noting three to five things you're grateful for in your journal each day. I've done a couple of podcast episodes that dive into how to do this effectively. Check out my podcast episodes relevant to gratitude practices in the Resources section at the end of this book.

Buffet Main Courses—Deeper Healing Treatments

The next section of your *Recovery Buffet* is composed of recovery methods that go deeper. These require more commitment and investment, but they can be profoundly helpful to your recovery. Think of engaging with these as being like going to the buffet for your main course; it's more of a commitment, but also more likely to satisfy your hunger for healing on a more profound level.

1. Therapy/Counseling

Therapy or counseling by a registered professional can be highly effective in your toxic-boss healing journey. Expressing your feelings to a therapist includes talking through your emotions like betrayal, anger, and sadness, and how you're feeling and thinking around what happened with your toxic boss. This will involve processing what happened so you can release negative emotions and energy, which is an important step in your healing. Working through your experiences in therapy can also help you to identify what you've learned from what you've gone through, as well as productive actions you can take going forward. Having an honest dialogue and learning healthier coping mechanisms through therapy is highly recommended.

As the title of "counselor" can be used widely and is generally not protected, be careful of working with a counselor or therapist who is not a registered professional. The danger of working with someone who is not professionally trained is that they will not be able to provide the evidence-informed treatment you need, and could actually do more damage than good in your recovery journey. Also important to note is the difference between a life coach and a therapist. A therapist is trained to help you understand your triggers and patterns of thoughts and feelings in relation to your toxic-boss scenario; coaches are not trained to work at this depth.

To ensure you get truly professional help, it's important that you work with a credible and educated professional therapist. Look for those with master's- or PhD-level training in counseling or clinical psychology. As licensing bodies vary across geographies, I've included a list of titles for professional therapists to look for in North America in the Resources section of this book.

Therapy is now widely available remotely (i.e., by private video platforms or phone), as well as in person. Choose the modality that best works for you. What's most important is the expertise, rapport, and fit of the therapist or counselor you select. It's helpful to do an initial inquiry or consult with more than one person to ensure you land on the best possible fit to help you heal from the impacts and trauma of your toxic boss. You'll find descriptions of some different therapy specializations you may want to explore in the Resources section of this book.

2. Medication to Support Your Mental Well-Being

If you are suffering from consistent anxiety and/or depression and your sleep is being impacted in a chronic way, it may be time to discuss a prescription from your family doctor or a psychiatrist. I purposefully put this after the counseling recommendations, as research has found that medication in combination with therapy is more effective in treating anxiety and depression than is taking medication by itself.

If you're struggling every day, a medication can help you better function and feel able to tackle other recovery items from the buffet. Some people strongly prefer to not take medication, however, and if you're one of them then it will be important to ensure you're utilizing as many of the other buffet items I listed in the Starters section as possible—especially exercise. Dr. John Ratey, a leading Harvard researcher on the brain and exercise, emphasizes how regular cardio can mimic the effects of an antidepressant. I spoke with him on my podcast about his book *Spark*, which explores how exercise is a great defense against depression and anxiety. (See the Resources section of this book to find this specific podcast episode.[3]) Other research has pinpointed dance as being particularly effective in improving emotional well-being and depression,[4] which makes sense, given that dance combines social interaction with movement and confidence building. Walking, jogging, yoga, and strength training have also been shown to be effective in treating depression. Further, the more intense level of exercise, the better the results/therapeutic effect.

Five months after having my third child, a beautiful baby girl, post-partum depression had me fast in its grip. This had happened after both of my sons' births, but this time was worse. I was in such an anxious and depressed head-space that the world around me seemed dark and I was convinced I would never feel like myself again. Each day was a grind, and my new business had struggled while I was off, forcing me to come back earlier post-partum than was ideal. Reasoning that this was a good distraction, I decided to attend a national conference that was important in my field of career development.

As I flew over Canada from west to east, a dark thought began looping in my mind; I'm embarrassed to say that I wished the plane would go down to end my misery. It was an intense and disturbing thought, and I can't believe I'm writing it now, but I wanted to share with you that I can relate if you're feeling dark thoughts and wish it would all just end.*

Tears filled my eyes and I turned toward the window so nobody could see them streaming down my cheeks.

That flight felt endless, but eventually we landed in Ottawa. I somehow faked my way through that conference. I knew I was depressed, as the darkness I felt wasn't getting any better and had lasted for many weeks.

When I got home, I went to my family doctor. I knew I needed medical help beyond the therapy, acupuncture, and herbal remedies I was using. She put me on an antidepressant, and within about ten days it was like I could see the light again—as if my dark shades had been removed and the world was gradually becoming brighter day by day. It

⇨

was remarkable, and to this day I'm grateful that this drug allowed me to feel joy and optimism again. It helped me to once again be the parent and business owner I wanted to be, both inside and out.

***Note** that wishing your life would end is suicidal ideation, and it's important to get help immediately. Even if you don't have a plan and these thoughts are fleeting, please get immediate help. There may be local distress resources in your area (see the Resources section for North American options).*

Buffet Desserts—Growth and Confidence Building

The final section of your *Recovery Buffet* includes recovery methods that will continue to help you build back your positivity and confidence once your healing is underway. These are not deep healing interventions like the main courses, but they will add to your recovery journey.

1. Personal Development

When I was reviewing stories that came in from research participants who'd successfully recovered from working with a toxic boss, it was clear that learning and development were common contributing factors to their well-being. "Developing" yourself means learning about and understanding what you have been through with a toxic boss, thereby strengthening yourself and your resilience moving forward. Here are some ideas for how to add self-development to your recovery journey:

- Write daily self-affirmations: Taking time each day to note in your journal what you're proud of or appreciate about yourself can make a big difference in how each day unfolds. Start each one with "I am . . ." and add a word that feels true to you. Examples are:
    - I am resilient
    - I am kind
    - I am creative
    - I am smart
    - I am loved

Once you have written these, state them aloud, ideally more than once, that day. As you're recovering, the more times you state these, the better. I've learned that if these are repeated daily (and multiple times a day) they will become part of your subconscious, literally sinking in. You will start to believe they are true.

> ***Remember who you are. All of your professional accomplishments are still there, and they're yours.***
>
> —DIRECTOR IN HIGHER EDUCATION
>
> ***A counselor gave me this tip—to ask myself each day, "What's really true about me?" and then answer in a few words in my journal (e.g., I am creative, resourceful, and good). This has helped me rebuild my confidence.***
>
> —HUMAN RESOURCES, TECH INDUSTRY

- **Help others who are working for a toxic boss:** A powerful way to heal from a toxic boss is to help others who are currently dealing with one. You now know way more than you did before, both from your lived experience and reading this book. You can be a source of support for someone navigating a toxic boss, which will help your own growth. In my opinion, there's no greater way to heal than to help another human to heal.

- **Read and learn about toxic bosses:** You are well into your learning process if you're reading this chapter—great job! Continuing to learn about toxic bosses through podcasts and articles can further help you understand that you're not alone on this journey. Reading or hearing about others who are now thriving post–toxic boss can make a big difference in your healing journey. My podcast *Where Work Meets Life*™ is a good place to start; you can find a list of these episodes, as well as blogs and articles, in the Resources section in the back of this book.

- **Join supportive online communities:** Communities exist that educate and provide support around toxic workplaces. Several such communities focus on workplace bullying, which has been dubbed a *silent epidemic* and public health threat and is estimated to impact over 79 million employees in the United States alone, either through directly being bullied or through witnessing it at work.[5] Examples of communities where you can find support include The Workplace Bullying Institute, The National Workplace Bullying Coalition, and the well-known online community of Glassdoor (see the Resources section for more details and links to each).

Dr. Laura's Coaching Break: *Obstacles to your toxic-boss recovery*

The buffet of recovery options is a lot to digest (pardon the pun!). Know that it's a gradual process to recover from a toxic boss, and successful healing involves trying different tools and strategies and seeing what works best for you.

There are certain obstacles that can get in the way of your recovery that you may need to address:

1. **Procrastination.** Do you find yourself putting off doing things for your recovery? Do you promise you will start the next day, or the next week, yet the days and weeks pass without you having taken any action?
2. **Low energy.** Do you want to get active and take steps for your recovery, yet you feel drained and simply don't have the energy to begin?
3. **Low mood.** Do you feel down, depressed, and simply not able to take any concrete actions to heal and lift your spirits?
4. **No time.** Are you in another job and finding that your work and life are too busy to take any time for your intentional healing? Is your schedule so full that you don't have time for yourself and your recovery initiatives?

List in your journal which of these obstacles are getting in your way, then see below for ways to combat each obstacle. As you review, note in your journal which of these you will try.

You can also add other recommendations from friends, loved ones, or a therapist or coach.

HOW TO OVERCOME THESE OBSTACLES:

Procrastination

1. Enlist a buddy to help hold you accountable, checking in on your progress and offering support and encouragement.
2. Start with one small thing each day that you will tackle, adding others on as you build momentum.
3. Create a schedule, much like the *personal wellness plan* we created in Chapter 4, that includes various recovery items, and spacing these out throughout your week to make them more doable.
4. To energize yourself to complete the items in your schedule, reward yourself in some small way for each task you accomplish.
5. Can you come up with some other ways to combat procrastination? (write these in your journal)

Low Energy

1. Do energy-building activities early in your day, which will help jumpstart your energy to carry you through each day. For example, exercise or walk in the morning.
2. Schedule breaks and downtime so that you can build energy between your appointments or tasks.
3. If you're working and depleted by the end of your workday, schedule your workout or a walk before work or during your lunch hour so you can build up energy earlier.
4. Can you come up with some other ways to combat low energy? (write these in your journal)

Low Mood

1. Which of your friends and family members lift your spirits when you talk to them? Book a conversation or coffee with one of these people each week.
2. If you are feeling depressed, address that through the recommendations earlier in this chapter. Until your depression is healed, it will be difficult to progress with your toxic-boss recovery.
3. Build in time for exercise and fresh air, which science has repeatedly shown is a great antidote to low mood due to the endorphin release it triggers. Doing so with a friend is highly recommended!
4. Can you come up with some other ways to combat low mood? (write these in your journal)

No Time

1. Examine what your weeks and weekends look like. Is there anything you can move from your plate or rebook to allow pockets of time for *you*?
2. Can you do small things, such as five minutes of breathing or meditation, for a quick break during your workday?
3. Talk to a loved one about ideas for building in more space for your recovery. They may think of resources and strategies that you haven't.
4. Can you come up with some other ways to combat a lack of time for you? (write these in your journal)

Finding a Healthier Work Situation

If you are already working in another job when you're reading this chapter, I hope that it's a much healthier workplace than your last; finding a better leader and work environment will help you further heal. Positive reinforcement from your new job will help rebuild your confidence. Working for a leader who is more trusting, collaborative, and supportive will be immensely helpful in the long run, although it will take time for you to rebuild your ability to trust.

> *[My new role] made me realize and appreciate good leadership and good organizational and work structure. My recovery did not feel very hard because I'm very fortunate to have found a new position with such understanding bosses who instilled trust and autonomy, which I thought I would never be able to have because I was so micromanaged before.*
>
> —LEGAL ASSISTANT
>
> *I found another job that was chill and supportive. During the hours that I did work, I was always doing things that I loved and collaborating with people whom I really appreciated.*
>
> —CONSULTANT

Recovering from a toxic boss is a marathon, not a sprint. You will need lots of support of various kinds, as well as time and patience, to get through this healing process. My hope is that the strategies in this chapter will equip you with the ability and tools to fully heal and empower you to repair any damage your toxic boss has done.

Takeaways from Chapter 6

- ✓ Working for a toxic boss has some similarities to being in a toxic romantic relationship and can lead to trauma symptoms that will require time and professional support to heal.
- ✓ Understanding the symptoms you are experiencing post–toxic boss is key in your healing journey. These include emotional symptoms (depression, burnout, anxiety), physical symptoms (muscle pain, gut issues, elevated blood pressure), behavioral changes (problems sleeping, unhealthy eating), and relationship impacts.
- ✓ There are many options for recovery, including therapy/counseling, medication, self-care activities, connection with others, mindfulness/meditation, journaling, and personal development.
- ✓ It's important to be aware of any obstacles to your recovery journey and implement strategies to address these.
- ✓ Ultimately, finding a healthier work situation will help you further heal and regain your confidence.

CHAPTER 7:

NEVER AGAIN! THE WARNING SIGNS OF TOXIC BOSSES

"The intuitive mind is a sacred gift and the rational mind is a faithful servant. We have created a society that honors the servant and has forgotten the gift."

—Bob Samples

Once you've experienced working for a toxic boss, you'll undoubtedly want to avoid getting into that situation ever again. This chapter will answer the question of how you can identify a toxic boss *before* accepting a job. You have learned a lot about toxic bosses and are equipped to tackle your healing and recovery journey. But to ensure you never get into a toxic-boss situation again, you need to become vigilant and knowledgeable about toxic-boss warning signs. This will help you move forward as you progress your career within or between organizations.

Cale had the unfortunate experience of having two toxic bosses in a row. He had advanced his career in the restaurant industry to the assistant manager level of a new and popular restaurant. He had worked hard to help open this unique restaurant and was proud of the exceptional reviews it had received over the past eighteen months.

The first general manager he worked for seemed great for the first few weeks, then proved to be a Self-Serving Egomaniac and Control Freak. The size of this man's ego was only matched by his extreme need to control every single detail in the restaurant. Just when Cale thought he couldn't take another day, this boss announced he was leaving to work for a more prestigious restaurant in a larger city. What a relief for Cale and the entire team . . . but brighter times did not lie ahead.

In a panic to get someone in quickly, the owner brought in his cousin, who had managed multiple businesses in the hospitality industry but never a restaurant. At first, she too seemed kind and hardworking. But rather than learn the ropes from those who had navigated the first year together as a team, she chose to do things her own way, and as a result proceeded to make ridiculous rookie mistakes, like under- or over-scheduling shifts. But the worst part was that she was a Dishonest Manipulator who pushed blame for each mistake onto the team so the owner (her cousin) would not realize she was the responsible party.

Further, as a Great Divider, she favored a few of the staff and pitted everyone in the team against one another. The restaurant had become an even worse place to work in than under the first boss. People no longer trusted each other, and going into work each day, Cale felt like he was walking on thin ice. ⇨

Exhausted from navigating two toxic bosses in a row, Cale was planning to quit, but he was worried about his ability to spot the signs of a toxic boss in other restaurants. What if he ended up working for one again? He couldn't imagine going through this a third time. It was beginning to feel like maybe all workplaces would be toxic, and he doubted his ability to detect the signs in his job search.

A lot of us have found ourselves in Cale's position after working for a toxic boss. The good news is, there are ways to detect the signs of a toxic workplace and a toxic boss. Understanding the signs of both a healthy and a toxic workplace culture will help you minimize your chances of entering into another toxic situation.

Searching for a Better Boss Starts with Seeking a Healthier Workplace

Toxic bosses are less common in healthy workplaces. In my experience, unhealthy or toxic workplace cultures enable toxic bosses to thrive, and in turn, as toxic bosses increase in number and influence, workplace cultures become increasingly toxic. The phrase "toxic workplace" is an abstract term to describe a variety of behaviors, including infighting, intimidation, and other upsetting situations in the workplace.[1]

According to McKinsey, toxic workplace behavior is interpersonal behavior that leads employees to feel unvalued, belittled, or unsafe, such as unfair or demeaning treatment, non-inclusive behavior, sabotaging, cutthroat competition, abusive management, and unethical behavior from leaders or coworkers.[2]

It's critical that you seek out healthy, positive workplaces as a starting point. Although these do not guarantee you won't come across a toxic boss, you are much less likely to find one if the overall culture of the organization you're entering into is a healthy one.

Dr. Laura's Coaching Break: *What does a healthy workplace look like for you?*

How do you find a *healthy* workplace? First of all, you need to be clear on what "healthy" specifically looks like for *you*. Although there are some common characteristics, we each have different expectations when it comes to our ideal workplace culture.

Here are a number of characteristics of healthy workplace cultures. Start by checking off those that are important to you in your next workplace, and add any others that come to mind:

- ❑ Respectful (people respect each other, including leaders respecting their people)
- ❑ Honest and open communication is expected across all levels
- ❑ Employee well-being is a priority
- ❑ Employee involvement and feedback are encouraged (e.g., annual engagement surveys are acted upon)
- ❑ Work–life balance is respected (e.g., taking vacation time is mandated, expectations are set about not replying to emails on evenings and weekends)
- ❑ Flexibility is supported (e.g., flexible work hours, ability to work a hybrid/remote setup)
- ❑ New ideas and perspectives are heard and considered

- ❑ Collaboration is expected (while competition is discouraged)
- ❑ Growth and development is supported and encouraged
- ❑ Recognition and appreciation for accomplishments and hard work is common
- ❑ Strong leadership is valued and supported, and employees have the opportunity to provide feedback on their manager/leadership
- ❑ Mental and physical health are supported through both conversation and generous benefits (e.g., EAPs/EFAPs, health insurance/benefits, stress management and wellness trainings, exercise access)
- ❑ Other healthy workplace characteristics that are important to you (note in your journal)

Are any of the items you checked off or listed here *non-negotiable* for you in your next workplace? Are any of these *nice to have* but not *critical*? Refer to this checklist throughout your job search and revisit it when making decisions about fit with a position and organization. Using your non-negotiables when it comes to workplace culture will help you make solid career decisions. In the following sections, I will share ways to evaluate whether these characteristics exist in the workplaces you're considering.

Sleuthing Workplace Cultures Online

Identifying the healthy workplace characteristics that you're looking for at your new position is only half the battle. You will also need to take steps to understand what the organization's culture is like before you work there, to make sure it's a fit. This means understanding if the positive characteristics you deemed important exist at the new company, as well as checking for indicators of a toxic workplace.

Company websites often give glowing descriptions of their values, but what's listed there may not always play out in real life. Likewise, when you interview and ask questions of HR or hiring managers, they may give you a rosy picture of their workplace that's aspirational rather than realistic, and may not reflect any negative or challenging aspects of their culture. It's critical that you get a clear sense of the positives *and* the challenges, so you can weigh how these fit your needs and non-negotiables and make an informed decision.

Looking at sites like Glassdoor can be helpful in identifying signs of a healthy or toxic workplace. Ratings of 3.5 stars and higher are considered "good," but it's also important to note if these have been declining over time. Specifically, the reviews over the past six to twelve months can be telling—are there many very negative reviews, such as a lot of 1-star ratings? Are certain words consistently mentioned, like *micromanagement*, *poor leadership*, or *lack of work–life balance*?

Some **key indicators of a toxic workplace** you should be on the lookout for are:

- Inappropriate behavior (harassment, bullying) is ignored or excused
- Expressing concerns is discouraged
- New ideas or opinions aren't welcome
- People feel like they're walking on eggshells
- Trust is lacking (between peers, with leadership)
- Employees are increasingly sick or on medical leaves

- Turnover is high
- Mistakes are punished rather than learned from
- Successes are not appreciated nor celebrated
- Favoritism is rampant in reward and promotion decisions

Job Descriptions: Looking for Hints at Culture and Values

When you are reviewing specific job descriptions for roles you're considering, be on the lookout for language that matches the healthy workplace culture descriptors you came up with earlier. For example, if you're looking for a supportive, respectful organization that values work–life balance and flexibility, do you see any of these descriptors, or something similar, in the posting?

You can even use AI prompts to help you analyze a job description. A sample prompt would be: "*Here's a job description. Can you analyze it and tell me if it suggests a supportive and respectful environment? Highlight any phrases or words that reflect these qualities.*"

Use the job descriptions you find as a starting point to investigate whether the company demonstrates these healthy workplace indicators or values in action, such as through employee testimonials or awards for best workplaces. Know that these awards are broad, however, and do not often drill down to the quality of specific leaders. Toxic bosses can still exist in organizations that are deemed *best places to work*. Still, the more positive evidence, comments, and reviews that exist online about an organization, the less chance there is that you'll meet a toxic boss there.

Word on the Street: Talking to Former Employees

In addition to sleuthing online, it's extremely helpful to talk with people who have worked at the organization and for the boss you're considering. Smaller or newer companies, for example, may not have as much of an online presence from which to sleuth information. Instead, try to speak with people who work there.

> *I really needed a job so I ignored the warning signs. I wish I would've spoken to the people who had gone before me and didn't last very long in the role. I should have asked more questions.*
>
> —HEAD OF PRODUCTION

You can gain access to these people through your network, by using a professional networking platform like LinkedIn, or by asking around your network for relevant contacts. Do any of your colleagues from past jobs know them? Do any of your friends, family, or neighbors have a connection to them? What about people you went to school with or trained with? Your network is bigger than you think, and oftentimes we are only one step removed from *someone who knows someone*.

Kaleem was excited when he saw the position posted. He had taken a medical leave from a toxic boss who was an Unethical Corruptor, among other things. His nerves and confidence had been shot, so he had taken a couple of months to focus on his healing before searching for his next opportunity. Now, through a combination of professional counseling, a strong support system of friends and family, time in nature, and his spiritual practices, Kaleem was beginning to feel more like his old self. He felt a flicker of optimism begin to burn inside; he had a renewed sense of optimism about landing somewhere much healthier. And the first week he began searching for his next opportunity, he came across a promising posting from a national tech company that had recently opened an office in his city.

He found a lot of positive information about the company online, including a Glassdoor score of 4.0, and the corporate values on their website spoke to what was also important to him. Running the job description through ChatGPT highlighted that the job description included terms like "collaborative team," "professional development opportunities," and "employee wellness programs," which suggested a focus on support and growth. This sounded promising, but his guard was up from his toxic-boss experience. He needed to speak with someone about what the new office and the boss he'd be working under were like.

He began sending messages on LinkedIn and emails to other people in the tech industry to see if anyone knew this potential boss or anyone else currently working for the company. He also found a second-degree connection on LinkedIn to someone who used to work for the firm in another city. In addition, he sent connection requests to a couple of people working there who had graduated from his alma mater.

These efforts led Kaleem to be introduced to two members of the team he would work with, as well as someone who worked for the same boss five years earlier in a different firm. Each conversation was informative and interesting. He learned that the company culture was hardworking and performance-focused, but that they treated their people well (which was one of the top characteristics he was looking for). They had a great health and wellness plan, and offered their employees flex days in addition to vacation days. They also trained on and supported mental health on a regular basis.

He also learned the boss he would report to was a family person who set boundaries in her work and home life and respected that everyone needed time for rest and rejuvenation. She took vacations where she fully unplugged, and she encouraged every member of her team to do the same. People who no longer worked with her still spoke highly of her as a key mentor in their careers. Although she had high expectations, she had people's backs and supported them to develop the skills they needed along the way.

All these signs pointed to a healthy boss and workplace culture, and by the time Kaleem was offered the role, he felt confident that this would not be another toxic-boss scenario.

How do you ask someone about their former role and boss? You may decide to do this while you're in the hiring process, or not until you have an offer. It needs to feel natural to you, and certainly not come across as pushy or nosy. Therefore, it's important to be transparent that you are considering a role and would like to know more about the person's experience as you determine if the company is a fit for you.

Here are some good ways to ask for this information:

- If you're open to sharing, I'd love to know—what was your former boss like to work for?
- I'm considering working for the same boss you reported to, and I'm wondering what they are like to work for. What are your thoughts?
- What were the best aspects and challenges of working for that supervisor?

Some people may be more closed than others about sharing information if it is negative, yet you'll be able to glean as much from what they *don't* say as what they do. If they respond awkwardly or say very little, it may suggest a less-than-ideal boss. Silence can indicate an undercurrent of negative experiences that they are simply not comfortable sharing. People who respect and appreciate their leader will have no problem sharing positives, such as how their boss was supportive, fair, a visionary, etc. If they left that job for a reason like a better opportunity rather than out of a desire to escape a toxic boss, this will come through as they describe their decision and path. Listen closely and observe their nonverbal cues, as well as what they say (which is why in-person or video is better than phone or text-based conversations in this regard).

When a workplace is toxic, word on the street points to this toxicity over time. The more people who have left disgruntled, the more word will spread about toxic conditions. You can learn which organizations in your industry are more toxic through having as many networking and social conversations as possible. If you are more introverted, this can be more challenging; you may find that having these conversations drains your energy. If that's your situation, try to space out such discussions and pace yourself in a way that's manageable for you. It's also okay to have conversations via video if face-to-face meetings feel too draining.

Conversations with Current Employees

Like former employees, current employees can also shed light on the healthiness of the workplace culture and on their boss. Because they are currently employed there and working for this boss, they are much less likely to give honest negative reviews if they are experiencing difficult or toxic behavior. Still, as with former employees, they are still worth asking, because it's as much about what they *don't* reveal as what they willingly offer up.

Here are some questions you could consider asking:

- How would you describe your boss in a few words?
- What are the best aspects and any frustrating aspects about your boss? (Note that they may only feel comfortable answering part one of this question, but see how the conversation goes.)
- Do you feel supported and encouraged?
- Do you feel respected and valued?
- Is the workplace inclusive?
- Is diversity valued and supported?

- Do you feel raises and promotions are decided upon fairly?
- Do you feel the workload is reasonable, or are you overloaded constantly?
- Do you have the level of flexibility you want?
- Is your growth and career development supported?
- Do you have access to benefits that support your physical and mental health?

Be sure to put these questions into your own words—and of course, the nature of the connection you have with the person you're asking will dictate how many of these questions to ask. Be sure to leave silence for them to consider their responses after asking each question. This gives the opportunity to contemplate their current scenario and talk about their work at greater length, which can be a win/win. Whether they say a lot or a little, any answers you get can help reveal what you may be getting yourself into.

If you happen to have the chance to see your potential boss interacting with others, such as at an event, be on the lookout for how they treat others. As one of my research participants aptly put it, "When you see them treating other people in a condescending way, know that this will be you one day!"

Warning Signs During the Hiring Process

Once you have applied and are recruited into the hiring process, you will have access to much more data about your potential boss, team, and workplace culture. If you found the role through a recruiter or placement agency, be sure to ask them about their knowledge of the leadership and workplace culture. Asking the recruiter the same types of questions you ask to current employees is an excellent strategy. Pay special attention to any answers that are similar or reconfirm what another party has already said.

> *I was getting uncomfortable vibes in my interview, but I urgently needed a job.*
>
> —ASSISTANT DIRECTOR IN HIGHER EDUCATION
>
> ....
>
> *When interviewing for jobs, I now look for transparent communication and also clear responsibilities and expectations.*
>
> —LEGAL ASSISTANT

Once you are in an interview, take note of each of these behaviors as warning signs of a toxic boss or workplace:

1. Dominating the Interview

Toxic bosses who fit into many of the 8 Toxic Boss Personas love the sound of their own voices and tend to talk much more than listen. Although they will ask questions, they much prefer talking about how great they are and how lucky you'd be to work for their organization. They will not allow you space to ask your questions, nor will they deeply listen to your responses. Consider this a warning sign and a taste of what's to come if you take the job. Likewise, if others interviewing you, such as HR or other decision-makers, dominate the conversation or appear egotistical, take heed of this as a warning sign.

Smile, nod, smile, nod . . . Shelley continued this pattern for almost the whole interview. The manager she would be reporting to would not stop talking—bragging about what an unbelievable team she'd built, the awards she'd won, and how much revenue she alone had been responsible for in her time with the company. Her questions for Shelley were few and far between, and as Shelley answered those rare queries, it was clear her potential boss was inching toward what to say next.

When Shelley left the interview, she knew this woman didn't know much about her. How on earth could she assess Shelley's fit for the role? Yet the offer came in the next day. Her nodding and smiling must have been signs of a good fit? Or, more likely, her agreeableness simply stroked this boss's ego.

As much as the work sounded interesting, Shelley knew that communication needed to be a two-way street: talking and listening. She saw this boss's lack of interest in listening as a negative sign and declined the offer.

2. Frequently Interrupting

As part of their dominating style, toxic bosses will frequently interrupt you—both to gain more airtime and because they don't value what you have to say. Interruptions can be an unavoidable part of virtual (e.g., Zoom or Teams) interviews due to time lags, but if they happen consistently, and if they happen in person more than once or twice, this could be a sign of a difficult or toxic boss. This also goes for others interviewing you from the organization. Healthy workplaces value what employees, including potential hires, have to say.

3. Disrespecting Your Time and Needs

The way you are treated and communicated with during the hiring process is a good indicator of your potential boss's style. Do they respect your time by only contacting you during business hours, or do they contact you in the evening or on the weekend *and* expect an immediate response? If you have asked about flexibility and hybrid work options, do they shut that down immediately or do they listen to your preferences and consider them, even if organizational policy may get in the way? Do they start and end the interview on time, respecting that your time is valuable?

Nick sat in the waiting room, nervously fidgeting as the minutes ticked by. His interview was supposed to have started twenty-five minutes earlier. He had been fifteen minutes early, a habit he'd formed that allowed a cushion of time to ensure he'd never run late. He'd used the extra time to take deep breaths and ground himself pre-interview. But this extended waiting period was unsettling.

When the boss finally came out, he made an excuse of how busy he was without apologizing for taking up so much of Nick's time. Then, during the interview, he took a phone call, saying it was an urgent business deal. That ate up another fifteen minutes. The interview lasted almost forty minutes past the time it was supposed to end, resulting in a parking ticket that was flapping in the wind on the windshield of Nick's Mini Cooper when he finally arrived back at his car.

As he drove away, Nick knew he couldn't report to a boss who had no respect for his time—it would not only be frustrating but also highly inefficient.

4. Silence or Awkward Responses About Their Leadership

One of the questions you should always try to ask at the end of an interview is what your potential boss's leadership style is like. The way they answer this question can tell you a lot. If their answer is humble and reflects self-insight, it's more likely they're a good leader. If, however, they are boastful and arrogant, bragging about what a great leader they are, take this as a warning sign of a toxic boss. Or, if they have trouble answering this question and there is an awkward silence, this may reflect a lack of self-insight and leadership development, and be a sign of a *difficult* boss.

The four signs we've just covered are what I like to call *red flags*, indicating a high potential of a toxic boss. The more of these indicators that are in play, the more you need to be aware of your risk.

In sum, the hiring process is like dating: You need to be aware of the signs that surface and how you are feeling. Does it make you want to go on a second date, or in this case a second interview, or to accept an offer? You should feel heard, respected, and appreciated every step of the way. Just like in dating, trusting your intuition is important; *so* important that the next section addresses this key topic, which was captured in the quote at the beginning of this chapter: "The intuitive mind is a sacred gift and the rational mind is a faithful servant. We have created a society that honors the servant and has forgotten the gift."

Trusting Your Intuition

Have you ever had a "gut instinct" or a "feeling" about a decision in your work or career that you wished you had trusted? When you think back to your last toxic boss, did you have a gut instinct that you ignored? Do you recall having that inner feeling and ignoring or excusing it away, only to later regret not acting upon it? Do you resonate with any of the thoughts below?

- *I had a feeling he wouldn't be a good boss, yet it was an offer I couldn't refuse that paid well and had opportunity for career advancement.*
- *I just had a sense something was off but I couldn't explain it, and my friends and colleagues were excited for me about this opportunity, so I decided to accept it.*
- *She said all the right things to welcome me on the team, but I just felt that something wasn't quite right; I had a feeling not to trust her.*

These feelings, hunches, or instincts are about our intuition speaking (or sometimes *screaming*) at us as we navigate the hiring process.[3] According to a recent article in *Psychology Today*, our intuition is a form of knowledge that enters into our consciousness automatically.[4] Our hunches or gut instincts are generated by our subconscious minds rapidly sifting through our wide array of past experiences and knowledge.[5]

Our intuition is especially sensitive to risks or harm a decision we are making right now could later subject us to, such as working for a toxic boss. Yet how often do we ignore our intuition in favor of the external data that we put far more value on? Quite often, indeed! Many of my clients and research participants explain that something felt "off" when they interviewed for a job that later went south, yet they went ahead and accepted the job anyway. They wish they had listened to their wise inner voice during the interview and job acceptance process.

Speaking of listening to your inner voice and instincts, one of my research participants recommended the book *The Gift of Fear*,[6] a title that one of my beloved mentors—my sister-in-law Kathleen—shared with me as a young woman, and that I too recommend regularly to others. As this participant said to me, "*The Gift of Fear* explains how we instinctually know things, then we use our rational brain to explain things away. And then it puts us in harm's way. We need to pay more attention to our gut reactions versus rationalizing them away. We shouldn't sell ourselves the fiction that everything is fine."

In this time of endless data, including trends, stats, big data, and AI, data is everywhere and is applauded as the direction the world of work needs to continue heading in. Human intuition, in comparison, is more often treated as emotional, biased, subjective, and inaccurate. Yet, according to Gerd Gigerenzer, a psychologist at the Max Planck Institute for Human Development in Berlin, intuition *is a form of unconscious intelligence that is as needed as conscious intelligence.*[7] Furthermore, *intuition can be not only faster than reflection but also more accurate.* Indeed, your brain makes more rapid connections than any computer can.

In sum, trust your intuition every step of the way as you explore organizations online, speak to others, and interview with your potential boss, HR, or anyone else in the company. Rather than suffer under a toxic boss, learn to allow space for and give respect to your intuition so that it can be a source of guidance and direction as you navigate whether to take on this next role. If your gut tells you something is off, pause, listen, and take heed.

Katy sat across from her parents, both boomers who had climbed corporate ladders in their careers. Katy was getting their advice about a promotion in her environmental services company. She would be a director reporting to a VP, which was a big and exciting promotion. This VP, however, was known to be challenging, and a few people had quit their unit in the past two years.

Katy explained to her parents that he was very complimentary about her skills and had charmed her into feeling needed in the position. Yet something about his demeanor and confidence made her stomach churn. She had a sense that something wasn't right, that he wouldn't be so nice once she was lured in. Her parents encouraged her to accept the position regardless, not understanding why she'd turn down a promotion of this level.

Katy went back home, and that evening she sat in her favorite armchair and took time to meditate, reflect, and journal about the decision and what her intuition was telling her. As she wrote down her thoughts and feelings, it became even clearer that there were warning signs and she needed to trust her inner voice. She had learned in her past that when she failed to do so, it always backfired later. Her career and well-being were too important to take this risk, regardless of the honor it was to be asked.

Much to everyone's surprise, Katy turned down the offer. Five months later, she was recruited to an even better role at another organization, where she worked for an incredible VP who would become her most valuable mentor throughout her career.

Turnover as a Trend

As you navigate your next opportunity, keep a close eye on what you learn about turnover or attrition in the organization or specific team you'd be working within. Toxic bosses are brutal to report to, and many of their employees don't last more than one to two years before leaving. They either quit, as it's simply not sustainable physically, mentally, and emotionally, or they are let go, as we explored in Chapters 4 and 5.

To find out if an organization has high turnover, you can ask your potential boss or those interviewing you about how long people have been on the team and how many have left in the past year or two. You can also inquire about turnover trends with current or past employees. In addition, searching LinkedIn may reveal whether people have moved on from that team.

This may not work for smaller companies or start-ups, as they likely don't have the longevity or past-employee numbers to be able to identify these trends. But in general, if you notice that many people have left a company, take it as a warning sign of a toxic environment. Toxic bosses are great at making excuses as to *why* people left (and none of the reasons have *anything* to do with their leadership).

If You Suddenly Find Yourself with Another Toxic Boss

One of the curveballs that's particularly difficult to navigate is when you find a healthy boss to report to, and then they leave the role and are replaced by a toxic one. Whether because of internal transfers, promotions, or moving on to better opportunities, there's no guarantee that your current boss will remain your boss. Hopefully it won't happen to you, but the possibility of a toxic boss coming up in your career is something worth being ready for. Like Margaret Thatcher said, "You may have to fight a battle more than once to win it"—and as mentioned earlier in this book, 87 percent of professionals have had at least one toxic boss during their careers, with 30 percent encountering more than one.[8] Hopefully you will not be in the 30 percent that gets stuck working for more than one, but the good news is you now have the knowledge, tools, and resiliency to cope and transition or exit much sooner.

Here are some pointers to follow if a toxic boss suddenly enters your world again:

- Avoid getting caught up in self-pity and how unfair your situation is. It's normal to feel frustrated, angry, cynical, or sad that this has happened to you *again*, but don't let yourself wallow for long. Instead, process those emotions by talking with trusted friends and loved ones, or, if you find your thoughts and emotions are bringing you down and stealing your motivation, find a therapist.

- Remember, you do have choices. Review the six options we covered in Chapter 3. Now that you understand all the nuances of navigating this situation, leaving (either by your choice or theirs), and recovering from a toxic boss, you will be better armed to make your choice more efficiently and effectively this time.
- Should you decide you need to leave, knowing that toxic bosses do not change and in fact almost always get worse over time, you should focus your energy as soon as possible on *creating a winning exit plan*, as covered in Chapter 4.

You now should be better positioned to spot the warning signs of a toxic boss and toxic workplaces in general. You've explored what a healthy workplace looks like, and how to increase your chances of ending up in one. If you do your research about possible future workplaces online, as well as talk to current and former employees, you will be much less likely to fall prey to a toxic boss again. There are warning signs in your interview process, and it's very important to trust your intuition. You can never guarantee that a toxic boss won't enter your work life again, but you are now more resilient and have the skills and tools to face and deal with this situation head-on.

Takeaways from Chapter 7

✓ Finding a great boss starts first with searching for a healthy workplace culture.

✓ It's important to explore what a healthy workplace looks like for you, as we all have preferences and values that can make our *non-negotiables* different.

✓ Sleuthing organizations online can help you spot early warning signs of a toxic workplace.

✓ Talking to former employees to learn the *word on the street* about an organization can be an informative step. Some may be disgruntled for reasons that you wouldn't be, so take every piece of feedback with a grain of salt, but look for patterns.

✓ Speaking with current employees is also a key step, and knowing what questions to ask can help you glean important information about the boss and workplace culture.

✓ Be aware of warning signs of a toxic boss during the hiring process.

✓ Remember to trust your intuition as it is a wise, inner voice that can guide you in avoiding a toxic boss or workplace.

CHAPTER 8:

THRIVING IN YOUR CAREER POST–TOXIC BOSS

"The best way to predict your future is to create it."
—Peter Drucker

You have come a long way on your toxic-boss recovery journey. Once you've implemented the strategies in this book, you'll be on the other side of the dark and difficult times, and busy rebuilding your career to be healthy and fulfilling. This is no small feat, and the resiliency you have built from going through this tough time will make you stronger moving forward.

This chapter will empower you to remain in the driver's seat of your career, to embrace the idea that the grass *can* be greener post–toxic boss, and to develop trust in your next workplace and leadership. Perhaps you're already working at your next job as you read this, or you're searching for your next opportunity. Either way, the stories from survivors embedded in this chapter will inspire you to thrive in your career and life post–toxic boss.

Empowering "You, Inc."

You are the Chief Executive Officer (CEO) of your own career. Nobody else will care as much about your career development as *you*. In generations past, especially the *traditionalist* generation (born 1928–1945) and generations prior, a person would most likely work at a single organization for their entire career. Switching jobs or careers was far less common, and people would depend on their company to fund and provide development for their career-related skills. There was more job security then, and in turn employees were more committed to their employers. Sure, there were toxic bosses back then, but people were more likely to grin and bear it. Their financial security required putting up with any poor treatment doled out, and an employee's mental health was not generally discussed at work or at home.

The world of work has evolved rapidly over the past century, and in the past few decades in particular, mergers, restructurings, and downsizings of companies have become the norm, not the exception. Salaries remain one of the biggest line items on a company's financial reports, meaning it's their largest expense. As a result, salaries are one of the first things executives look at when they are tasked with eliminating costs.

Humans can easily become numbers on a spreadsheet and can be laid off (let go without cause) from a company by getting *packaged out*. A package usually includes a severance, which is extra weeks, months, or even years of pay beyond the employee's termination to help them get by as they find new employment. The longer you have been working at the organization, the bigger the severance typically is.

Many people who are *boomers* (born 1946–1964), *Generation Xers* (born 1965–1980), *millennials* (born 1981–1996), and the newest generation to hit the workplace, *Generation Z* (born 1997–2012), have experienced layoffs themselves or seen colleagues or friends going through these tough times. In turn, they understand that job security is never a given, and therefore loyalty or commitment to any one employer is not usually strong on their end.

Empowering "You, Inc." means taking the driver's seat and proactively managing your own career so that when a curveball like an economic downturn or layoffs at your company is thrown, you can more easily pivot. "You, Inc." can build a network of allies, a portfolio of skills, and the confidence to navigate to your next career destination (whether that's a new job, contract work, or your own business) with minimal interruption. Let's explore why it's key to nurture your network of allies, grow your portfolio of skills, and gain confidence to navigate to your next career destination.

Nurturing Your Network of Allies

The word *networking* makes many people feel uncomfortable. Networking may bring visions of a salesperson pushing themself on others with unwanted asks (for example, cold calling). Many people, perhaps you included, don't like the thought of *selling* themselves, and worry that people are too busy to meet with them. Even while unemployed, you may be apt to avoid networking or keep it to a minimum—and when you're gainfully employed, you may feel no need whatsoever to network or keep up with outside professional connections, instead focusing your energy on your current job and colleagues.

If this sounds like you, beware, as this approach will not serve your career development in this rapidly changing work landscape. If you are not keeping up with outside relationships and nurturing your network of allies, you are going to have way more work to do and time to spend when you *do* need to pivot during a planned or unplanned transition.

I like to differentiate between *networking* and *ally building*, and I encourage my clients and audiences to focus on the latter, as it's a far more sustainable strategy for your career development:

- ***Networking*** is growing your connections to help you develop your career (typically when you are searching for a job).
- ***Ally building*** is developing two-way, longer-term relationships, and is done continuously throughout your career, not just when you're searching for work.

The following table compares and contrasts these two concepts:

NETWORKING	ALLY BUILDING
• Typically used when you're searching for work.	• Used consistently, not just when you're looking for a job.
• Sometimes comes across as selling yourself.	• A two-way relationship: you and another party learning about each other.
• Asking the question, *How can another person help me?*	• Asking the question, *How can the two of us help one another?*
• Pitching yourself to others.	• Listening to and sharing useful information, ideas, connections from and with others.
• Making the assumption that only people in positions of power (e.g., managers who could hire you) offer value.	• Being open to the fact that anyone, at any level, can offer value.
• Its purpose is to find you a new job.	• Its purpose is to give and receive information or support (two-way).
• Can lack a focus on your longer-term relationship building.	• All about building and maintaining relationships in an ongoing way, not just when you need them.

As you can see, ally building is about two-way relationships that you develop and maintain over time. These relationships are not just about needing something, such as a job, but about sharing information and supporting one another. You can build allies with people more experienced than you in their career, at the same stage as yourself, or with those just starting out.

People from each of these groups will give you certain gifts and receive certain gifts from you.

- Someone further along in their career receives the gift of giving you guidance to help you progress your career or potentially find a new job.
- Someone at the same career stage as you can be a support, a sounding board, share resources, or offer connections from their network (and vice versa!).
- Someone more junior than you in their career path gives *you* the gift of giving back—to provide your insights and learnings, and to make connections that can help them progress in their career. Essentially, you can pay it forward, which feels good. Don't underestimate the power of someone junior being able to help you through introductions and supporting your career journey, either. It can and does work both ways.

Giving and receiving from allies over the course of your career is all part of what I refer to as a *karmic system* of ally building that will ultimately help and empower you through the ups and downs of your career journey. By *karmic system*, I'm referring to the idea that what goes around, comes around—that the actions you take to help others will come back to you in different ways. I've seen this time and time again in my own life and in those of my clients.

Nathan was losing hope about finding another job after being laid off by his toxic CEO in an avionics company. The economy wasn't good, and being in his early fifties made it harder to find roles at the more senior leader level he wanted to continue at.

He had always taken the time to mentor others more junior in their careers. No matter how busy he was, if a new engineer or a student wanted to ask him about his career path, he would make the time. Among his direct reports, he was known as a leader who mentored them and helped them to grow and develop their careers. He was generous with his time and made them feel supported and inspired.

When Tracy messaged him on LinkedIn, he was happy to see her name. He remembered her as an ambitious and hard-working engineer in training (EIT) that he'd supervised nearly twenty years earlier for three years. Tracy had seen he was "Open to Work" on LinkedIn, so wanted to share a senior leadership role that she thought would be perfect for him at the company where she was a leader. She knew that his leadership style and values would fit well in her company's culture, which cared about people and was high-performing.

After Nathan landed the role, he expressed to Tracy how grateful he was. She replied, "Nathan, if it wasn't for your belief in me earlier on, I'd never have made it so far in my career. I'm delighted we can both be leaders here, and I know I will continue to learn from you!"

Your Portfolio of Skills

Think about the skills you have developed thus far in your career. Imagine you have a portfolio or briefcase where you collect these skills and carry them with you from job to job. These might be job-specific or transferable skills.

1. Job-Specific Skills

Your specific skills are the technical skills you've developed to do a particular job, such as using a programming language, operating a piece of equipment, or negotiating a contract. Building these skills required specific training or education. In the ever-evolving world of work, as technology changes, you must continue to upgrade your specific skills.

Always be on the lookout for which skills you could be developing; take the lead by asking your employer about supporting specific training, courses, certifications, or conferences as part of your career development. You cannot depend on your boss to look out for your development opportunities, as you are the CEO of "You, Inc." and must take responsibility for keeping your skill base current.

Have a conversation about your skills development at minimum once a year, during your annual development planning. If your company doesn't have an annual review process, you will need to bring it up on your own. If you ask and your employer is reluctant to support your skill development (for example, they refuse to pay for courses or will not allow paid time to pursue training), this may be a sign that your workplace isn't supportive of your career growth. If this is the case, you will need to ask yourself whether you want to stay.

2. Transferable Skills

Transferable skills are skills that are not specific to one type of occupation or sector, and can be transferred between jobs and industries. Examples include:

- Communication
- Problem-solving
- Project management
- Decision-making

Depending on your career, these may be even more important than your specific skills. These can be developed through training, coaching, mentorship, on-the-job experience, or other methods, and are part of your career development. Note that some transferable skills may be referred to as "soft skills." In my experience, these soft skills can be harder (no pun intended!) to develop than job-specific skills as they require a mixture of self-insight, emotional intelligence, empathy, listening, and other skills that can prove very challenging for some to master.

Larger and more sophisticated organizations may offer transferable skills–related training on a regular basis in-house, supported by learning and development departments. Smaller organizations typically will not bring in this training very often, so getting it outside will be necessary.

Just like when planning to build specific skills, having a conversation with your boss about how you can continue to develop your transferable skills is important. Whether your employer chooses to support or encourage your development will show you what type of leader they are and what kind of organizational culture you work within.

The clearer you are about your current and desired portfolio of specific and transferable skills, and the more you continue to develop these inside and outside of your employer, the more employable you will be as you continue to drive your career forward. This includes whether you're navigating unplanned transitions, or intentional career pivots, where you decide it's time to seek out another opportunity that will allow you to better grow.

Maya was in a sales account manager role in her organization. She had always been drawn to Human Resources (HR), but didn't know how she could make that pivot. She came across a certificate program in HR that she could work on in the evenings and weekends. Her colleague encouraged her to talk to her boss about it, on the off chance that the company might support it in some way.

She was nervous that her boss might see this as Mayá not being dedicated to her account manager role. But because she had built a trusting relationship with her boss—which had taken a couple of years after recovering from her last toxic boss (who, luckily, had left the organization)—she decided to take the idea to him.

Maya explained to her boss how interested she was in HR and about the certificate she planned to take. To her delight, he was not only supportive but was excited for her.

"We believe in developing our people and we'd rather keep you here and allow you to follow your interests than risk losing you," he told her. "We do have HR roles come up, and I'm going to get approval to pay for 50 percent of your certificate program. I know some of the skills will be useful in your current work, and that you will make an excellent HR professional one day."

Maya went on to successfully complete the HR certificate and, eventually, to secure an HR role in the company—but not before training her successor and leaving the accounts

⇨

she managed in excellent hands. A true win/win, and something that Maya will pay forward by encouraging other employees to follow and develop their interests as she moves into HR leadership.

Your Career Confidence

It takes confidence to sit in the driver's seat of your career, seizing the opportunity to be the CEO of "You, Inc." It means celebrating your successes and being proud of your accomplishments. Once your time working for a toxic boss is in the rearview mirror, rebuilding your confidence will be a priority. Know that if you put in the effort, you *will* arrive in a much better place!

By taking a risk and trusting that there were better leaders and better opportunities out there, I proved to myself that I could, above all, trust myself to make the right decisions for me and stand on my own two feet. Not only did I leave a toxic situation that was harming my well-being and quality of life but I found myself on a much better career path, in an organization with many inspiring leaders devoted to mentorship and coaching and developing talent. I have experienced so much growth and development in that time, both personal and professional, and I'm so grateful that I believed that the

⇨

> *grass could be greener on the other side—and that, frankly, it could be greener than I even had the ability to envision at the time. So here I am, still standing on my own two feet, and feeling more capable of forging the right way forward for myself than I have ever felt.*
>
> —MANAGER IN INTERNATIONAL CONSULTING FIRM

Dr. Laura's Coaching Break: *How have you grown from your toxic boss experience?*

Now it's time to reflect on the learnings and things you accomplished through what was likely one of the most difficult periods of your career (and possibly even your life). On the following page is a table to capture each learning or accomplishment, and how you can channel each experience to help you to thrive in your career moving forward.

As I've shared, I, too, have struggled when working for toxic bosses (the Ice Queen and others), so I've included a couple of examples from my own experience here to help guide you. Depending on where you're at in your recovery, you may still find it difficult to come up with any positive takeaways. I encourage you to keep coming back to this exercise in your journal in the coming weeks and fill it in as more accomplishments, however small, come to mind.

Start with recalling one of the challenges you experienced with your toxic boss. Next, pull out what you learned from this, or some aspect of the way you navigated it that you're proud of. Finally, describe how it will help you in your career moving forward.

Let's get started:

THE TOXIC BOSS	WHAT I LEARNED OR AM PROUD OF	HOW WILL THIS HELP ME THRIVE
challenge I experienced	*from navigating a toxic boss*	*in my career moving forward*
My toxic boss didn't have my back on an important decision when I needed her to. I was heartbroken and felt unsupported and untrusted.	*I am proud that I trusted my instincts and resigned (took a leap of faith) when I knew I couldn't take any more of my toxic boss not having my back.*	*I now know I have the answers within me when it comes to my career decisions. I am resilient and willing to take a leap of faith and a risk, even when I'm going through a terrible time.*
My toxic boss's leadership style didn't fit with my values (I went into this role without doing much due diligence when it came to understanding my boss's leadership style).	*I learned to be much more vigilant about who I work with and for, taking the time to collect and scrutinize information from others who have reported to them.*	*Resigning without a plan felt like a huge risk at the time, but I'm glad that I bet on myself. This has helped me avoid working with and for other toxic people. It also helped me believe in myself and that I can build a career that allows me to be the best I can be. I now am able to help people all over the world to navigate toxic bosses.*

Your answers . . .
(you can write them on the next page or in your journal. ⇨

THE TOXIC BOSS	WHAT I LEARNED OR AM PROUD OF	HOW WILL THIS HELP ME THRIVE
challenge I experienced	*from navigating a toxic boss*	*in my career moving forward*

More Ideas to Build Your Confidence Post–Toxic Boss

1. Find a Mentor

Find a mentor who can help you proactively navigate your career and take on opportunities that will grow your confidence. A mentor can inspire, guide, and impart wisdom from their career journey, and be a key part of your career development. Some organizations have formal mentorship programs to take part in, whereas many do not. If yours doesn't have a mentorship program, you can seek mentors either internally or externally who are willing to meet with you every month or two and spend an hour talking with you and offering you invaluable advice. I've included some tips for obtaining a mentor in the Resources section.

2. Be a Mentor

Giving back to others can be tremendously helpful to your own growth and confidence. Focusing on the challenges and development of someone that you can help will boost your good feelings about yourself and how far you've come in your own career journey. Further, you might end up with new, creative ideas that will help you in your own stage of career growth.

3. Get a Career Counselor or Coach

A career counselor or coach can help you develop your confidence post–toxic boss. Look specifically for a career counselor or career coach who has the experience and insights to help guide you toward expansion and growth in your career and can hold you accountable for taking action. Career counselors and coaches can help you navigate and build your career in your current organization and beyond.

4. Join Committees or Task Forces in Your Workplace

Committees or task forces help broaden your experience and add to your achievements. These experiences can grow your confidence and expand your perspective beyond your current role. They are also a way to practice ally building.

5. Join a Volunteer Committee in Your Industry Association

Most industry associations have opportunities to volunteer within. These types of committees increase your skills and broaden your network of allies, while at the same time developing confidence in yourself by giving back to others.

6. Try Things That Push You Out of Your Comfort Zone

Each of our comfort zones differ, with some of us liking more risk than others. One area many people find daunting is public speaking. As such, joining a public speaking community such as Toastmasters can be a great way to develop confidence. Or consider joining a group or club where you don't know anyone and will be forced to build new relationships and find new allies. Another idea is to take on a leadership role in a nonprofit community organization or club. Many people who take on these experiences are grateful for the growth they bring, even though they can be nerve-racking at first.

Raina was painfully shy. She always had been the quietest in her classes growing up. She dreaded meeting new people or being in the spotlight. She studied computer programming in college and ended up working her way into a large tech company, where her career was going well . . . until she found herself working under a toxic boss. Her confidence was shattered by this Control Freak who did not give her an iota of trust.

When Raina could no longer take her toxic boss, she quietly found another position and gave her notice. She knew she needed to build back her confidence as she no longer felt good enough, so she took a leap and joined an organization focused on building interest in STEM careers for young women. This required her to speak in front of hundreds of high school students. She was terrified but felt deeply supported by the executive director of the association, who provided her with mentorship on speaking to an audience and being herself versus trying to be somebody she wasn't.

As a result of this mentorship, Raina came across to her audiences as authentic and relatable. She even brought in her dry sense of humor. The students found her inspiring, and in turn, Raina felt her confidence begin to bloom. This carried forward to her workplace, where she put herself forward to speak more to audiences of employees and clients. She became noticed as a high performer and future leader, and her nontoxic boss promoted her to Team Lead the next year.

Developing Trust in Your Next Workplace and Boss

Working for a toxic boss and not being supported by your workplace to address this will leave you less trusting of your next boss. My research participants wondered how they could ever trust a boss or employer again. Many spoke about the lingering aftereffects of working for a toxic boss, such as being hypervigilant and having difficulty trusting other leaders. (Hypervigilance in this case means not taking anything your boss says at face value and assuming the worst, therefore exhausting yourself by actively protecting yourself with rigid boundaries on a daily basis.)

Even if you're someone who typically easily trusts others, working for a toxic boss erodes your ability to trust future leaders. Recognizing and understanding your *personal trust meter* will help you as you navigate building trust with your next boss. Trust is a key part of a strong and healthy two-way relationship with any boss—and it is something worth building, even if you find doing so difficult.

Krista's brain was on overdrive as she sat at her first one-on-one with her new boss. He was helpful, supportive, and encouraging, but Krista could not help but wonder . . . Was he really this way, or was it a façade? Would he turn into an Abusive A-Hole in the coming weeks or months, like her last boss had? Did he truly care about her growth in the company, or was he just saying what she wanted to hear?

As these questions churned in Krista's mind, she felt her pulse quicken and her palms sweat. She tensed up, feeling an urge to protect her inner self from future abuse. When he asked her about herself, she kept the conversation to business, not divulging much about her interests outside of work. She was determined to keep her work and life completely separate this time. Letting her last boss in on her personal life had been a mistake, as he'd turned it around in her face when his true colors emerged. Once he'd even said, "Krista, your work is slipping. You're probably spending too much time with your mother. Yes, she's elderly, but I hired you to be focused and to produce, not to be distracted by anything outside of work."

Her eyes had stung with tears when he'd said that. He had initially seemed genuinely concerned about her mother's dementia, so she had trusted him and opened up, telling him how challenging it was to watch her mother forget everything, including who Krista was. To then throw her mother's dementia in her face had felt like the biggest betrayal. Plus, when he said this to her she had been working fifty-five-hour weeks in her role as a project coordinator at their busy tech start-up. She wasn't spending nearly the time with her mother that she wanted to, and still her work efforts weren't enough for her toxic boss.

This history was why she couldn't imagine letting this new boss know anything personal—especially about her mother. She needed to protect her heart from being shattered again.

Think of your *trust meter* as a continuum that ranges from low trust to high trust. It reflects how likely you are to trust someone new to you at work; are you quick to trust, or do you distrust them until proven otherwise? Krista's *trust meter* in the story I just shared was, clearly, very low, meaning she couldn't trust others easily.

Use the following continuum to rate your own personal trust meter:

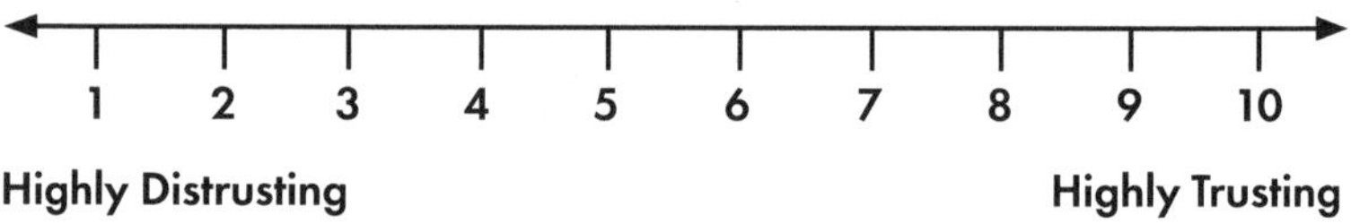

- **Highly Distrusting** (0–3)—Your natural inclination is to not trust people. You do not give your trust until someone proves themself. You are guarded and share little.
- **Moderately Trusting** (4–7)—You are somewhat trusting in a new working relationship, balancing caution with some initial trust, which is carefully given.
- **Highly Trusting** (8–10)—You assume people are trustworthy until they prove otherwise, and are quick to give them your trust.

Our propensity to trust is shaped both by our genetics and the people we grow up around. For example, if you come from a cultural background where conflict and distrust in society and government runs high, you are more likely to be naturally distrusting. Your trust meter was likely also influenced by what your parents and family had to say about trusting people in your formative years.

In childhood, were you told any of the following types of messages about trusting others?

1. *Don't trust anyone—the only person you can trust in life is yourself.*
2. *Be careful not to trust someone until they prove they can be trusted.*
3. *People can't be trusted; most people are only out for themselves.*

If you were told these or similar messages growing up, chances are your trust meter is on the lower side to begin with. Knowing this, it will naturally take you longer to develop trust in any boss, but will be 100 percent harder for you after having worked for a toxic one. Even if you were more easily trusting before your toxic boss, chances are your trust meter will have decreased through this experience.

Here are some of the behaviors that highly distrusting employees may have and how each can impact relationship development and productivity in their new jobs. Can you relate to any of these?

1. You keep your cards close to your chest.

You are nervous about sharing anything personal, so you don't develop relationships with your boss or anyone on your team, treating each person professionally but not showing any interest in their lives and hobbies beyond work. Because of this you are perceived as cold and detached, and are not involved in the collaboration and discussion that naturally occurs during working time and on breaks. This gets in the way of your ability to truly connect with your colleagues and be part of the team.

2. You have a propensity for setting rigid boundaries. Your toxic boss violated your boundaries at your last job. So now you set extremely rigid boundaries, such as only doing the exact tasks in your job description and not being adaptable or open to doing anything else. Although boundaries are important, overly rigid ones can make you difficult to work with, especially in an entrepreneurial or fast-growing company where you may need to wear different hats and pivot with changing needs. If your boundaries are too rigid it will limit what you can deliver in terms of helping your boss and colleagues, and in turn impact how they will help you.

Seth was determined to set strong boundaries at the outset of his new administrative assistant role. His former toxic boss had frequently contacted him after working hours and abused his personal time continuously. He remembered many vacation days sitting by the pool answering his boss's urgent calls that could have waited or been redirected. Hence, in this new job he turned off any way to reach him after hours and refused to give his personal cell for emergencies.

Three months into Seth's new job, something came up after hours that was truly urgent, and because of the boundaries Seth had put in place, a critical project was put in jeopardy. Seth felt terrible afterward, as all his boss needed from him was a quick answer to a key question, and instead his purposeful unavailability caused undue stress and productivity loss for his boss and team.

Ultimately, Seth's rigid boundaries will limit his enjoyment of work, his relationships with his boss and colleagues, and potentially his overall career growth and advancement. Working on increasing his personal trust meter, on the other hand, will unlock new opportunities for growth and success.

3. You have perfectionist tendencies.

You are so nervous about doing things perfectly that you're now triple-checking your work. Ever since your *Control Freak* toxic boss demoralized you for an accounting error, perfectionism has set in, and you are terrified of making a mistake. The result is that you are much slower at delivering and are weighing down your whole team.

These are just a few examples of how your level of distrust can impact your onboarding at a new job and your ability to build relationships with your new boss and team. You can, of course, choose to be highly distrusting and set up walls around yourself to avoid getting hurt or taken advantage of. But know that if you do this there may be impacts on your ability to fit in the team and culture, which could ultimately impact your growth and opportunities.

To build your trust meter, take the time to get to know the people you work with. As difficult as it may be, give them the benefit of the doubt. Take small steps toward learning key things about them, and share small things about you as you slowly develop these new relationships. Opening yourself up will take time and patience, and some risk, but will serve your career growth and teamwork better than will remaining closed to and distrusting of those you work with.

I've hired several employees into my businesses over the years who came from toxic workplaces. On more than one occasion, when I sensitively asked about what their last workplace or boss was like, tears filled their eyes. They were clearly still recovering from the trauma of a toxic boss, and despite being in a job interview, the way I empathetically asked the question made them feel safe to divulge the truth. Immediately after they shared that their boss was an *Abusive A-Hole* or *Control Freak*, the interviewees flushed red with embarrassment and apologized for sharing this. I assured them I understood and there was no judgment, and after being hired each one turned out to be an amazing, hardworking, loyal employee who thrived in the positive, caring culture of my firm.

The Grass Can Be Greener Post–Toxic Boss

Many of my research participants have shared with me that after leaving their toxic bosses, healing, and rebuilding, they have ended up in healthy and positive organizations and working for supportive bosses.

> *Working in a supportive organization with humble, kind, and collaborative leaders has reminded me that there are good leaders out there. The positive reinforcement has really helped me.*
>
> —MANAGER AT AN ENERGY COMPANY

It feels so good to know that people trust you and value your opinion! My new environment is caring and compassionate and my new manager is trusting.

—ADMINISTRATIVE COORDINATOR

I'm proud of staying the course. I explored my options and didn't make rash decisions. This has been a fifteen-month journey. Extricating myself took a lot of exploration and required patience. I explored all my options, including partnering with other people to move my career forward.

—MANAGING EDITOR

My new organization [post–toxic boss] made me realize and appreciate good leadership and good organizational and work structure.

—LEGAL ASSISTANT

It's the best decision I could have made to take on my current role. I've been there eight months. Trust is wildly different than at my toxic workplace, where they would take credit for your ideas. They hire the correct people to do the correct job here. Then they trust. They support you when you make a decision, they give feedback and you feel supported. They trust you to run your department and give positive and constructive feedback, and never make you feel ashamed.

—FOOD AND BEVERAGE OPERATIONS MANAGER

Takeaways from Chapter 8

- ✓ You are the CEO of your own organization—"You, Inc."—and must proactively manage your career so that when curveballs hit you can navigate them successfully.
- ✓ Networking and ally building are not the same things, and the latter is a far more sustainable strategy for your career development.
- ✓ Nurturing your network of allies is essential in this rapidly changing work landscape.
- ✓ Your portfolio of skills that you carry through your career includes both specific and transferable skills. As you navigate your career, be on the lookout for what skills you need to be developing to remain employable; do not depend on your employer to do this for you.
- ✓ Developing confidence is key to thriving in your career post–toxic boss; celebrate your successes and be proud of your accomplishments.
- ✓ Consider finding a supportive mentor or coach, joining committees or task forces, taking courses that push you out of your comfort zone, or joining a volunteer committee in your industry association as you work to rebuild your confidence.
- ✓ Building trust in your next boss can be difficult and requires understanding your *personal trust meter*. Trust is important to your working relationship with your new boss, so if you currently have a low trust

meter, that's something you may want to work on, as it can impact your onboarding and relationships with your boss and team.

✓ The grass *can* be greener post–toxic boss, so a healthy and positive organization is likely in your future if you're not there already.

RESOURCES

Throughout the book, there were areas where I wanted to share more than what I could fit into a given chapter, including tools and resources to allow you to dive deeper into your development and recovery from working with a toxic boss; you'll find those extras here. You will be able to come back to this Resources section as needed on your journey—I hope you find it empowering.

Tips for Finding a Mentor

A mentor is a more experienced and trusted advisor who provides you with guidance, support, encouragement, and wisdom. If your organization has a mentorship program, start there and see whether it will meet your needs. If not, consider these options:

- Set up a mentoring relationship for yourself. If you take this route, first determine why you are seeking a mentor, and what type of mentor you are hoping for (e.g., are you driven to become a leader, therefore having a mentor who is a successful leader in your field or industry will be key?).

- Consider asking your HR advisor for ideas of possible mentors in your organization.
- For external mentors, ask your network of allies for ideas and suggestions.
- Use LinkedIn to find potential mentors in your field by connecting with people in your industry and engaging with their posts.
- Join associations in your industry where you can meet potential mentors by attending events and interacting in their online communities. Some will have formal mentorship programs as part of your membership.
- Be specific about what you hope to learn from a potential mentor. Start by asking for a meeting to ask them questions about their career journey, letting them know how you admire what they've achieved and would like to learn from them. If you have good rapport, you can then ask if they'd be willing to meet, say, every couple of months for an hour—either virtually or for coffee, breakfast, or lunch (your treat!)—for the next year as a mentor.
- If they say no because they are too busy, don't take it personally. Keep trying for another mentor. Mentorship is a gift not only to you but also to the person who has the opportunity to mentor you.

Podcast Episodes Noted in the Book

For those of you who appreciate listening to podcasts, I've selected key episodes from my show, *Where Work Meets Life™, with Dr. Laura* that provide additional information to help you navigate your toxic-boss journey and your recovery. I've organized these by topic area to make them easy to find.

All episodes can be found at www.drlaura.live/podcast, as well as on your favorite streaming platform (i.e., Apple, Spotify, etc.) or YouTube (search for *Where Work Meets Life*).

How to Thrive Under a Difficult Boss

- *Episode 83: Managing Your Boss: How to Succeed, Thrive, or Know When to Leave*

Navigating Narcissistic Bosses

- *Episode 35: Disarming the Narcissist at Work*
- *Episode 36: Navigating Narcissism in Work and Life*
- *Episode 37: How to Handle Narcissistic Personalities on the Job*
- *Episode 38: Healthy to Destructive: Exploring Narcissism in Ourselves and Others*

Healing and Recovering from a Toxic Boss

- *Episode 9: Grateful Leadership: The Road to One Billion Happier People*

- *Episode 39: Life's Messy, Live Happy: Keys to Contentment*
- *Episode 57: The Power of Exercise to Optimize your Brain and Mental Wellness*
- *Episode 61: Vitamin N: The Power of Nature in Work/Life Wellness*

Supportive Online Communities

As you navigate your journey, you may find it helpful to join online communities that can educate about and provide support around toxic workplaces, including communities that focus specifically on bullying. Here are some recommendations to check out:

- *The Workplace Bullying Institute* offers resources for employees and employers to recognize and address bullying behaviors (check out their YouTube channel at https://www.youtube.com/@WBI).
- *The Workplace Psychological Safety Act* focuses on ending workplace abuse (https://endworkplaceabuse.com/workplace-psychological-safety-act/).
- *The National Workplace Bullying Coalition* is another organization dedicated to raising awareness about workplace bullying and advocating for stronger legal protections for workers. They work to influence legislation and provide resources for affected employees. Find them at www.workplacebullyingcoalition.org or follow them

on LinkedIn at www.linkedin.com/company/national-workplace-bullying-coalition.

- *Glassdoor* is another popular community for people who have worked for toxic bosses. Specifically, this platform offers insights into company cultures, including toxic bosses, and helps individuals make informed career decisions. Glassdoor receives visits from over 55 million unique users each month and has amassed over 297,000 followers on their LinkedIn page as of February 2025. There is a community on Glassdoor called Surviving a Toxic Workplace, where thousands of members gather to share their experiences of toxic workplaces and offer support. (www.glassdoor.com/Community/surviving-a-toxic-workplace)

Finding Professional Therapists

If you're headed down the therapy route to process your feelings while recovering from a toxic boss, congrats! When looking for a therapist to support your toxic boss healing process, look for a registered or certified professional. These professionals have the right level of training and are bound by a code of ethical requirements to be a trusted helper.

Here are some reputable titles to look for in North America, which will vary based on your geographical location:

- *Registered Psychologist*
- *Registered Psychotherapist*

- *Registered Counseling Therapist*
- *Certified Clinical Counselor*
- *Certified Counselor*
- *Certified Mental Health Counselor*
- *Licensed Psychological Associate*
- *Licensed Professional Counselor*
- *Licensed Mental Health Counselor*
- *Licensed Clinical Professional Counselor*
- *Licensed Clinical Mental Health Counselor*
- *National Certified Counselor*

Therapy Specializations

As you interview potential therapists, here's a list of therapeutic specializations/modalities that can be useful when healing from a toxic boss, and what they entail. These represent a sampling of some key therapies so you can explore further and determine what's the best fit for you:

1. Trauma-Informed Therapists/Trauma Specialists

Some psychologists and therapists specialize specifically in treating trauma. Toxic bosses often cause traumatic impacts, and certain therapy modalities are effective at treating these impacts. Some of these are:

- **Eye Movement Desensitization and Reprocessing (EMDR).** Helps process and reframe traumatic memories through guided eye movements or other forms of bilateral stimulation. I tried EMDR myself when I was struggling with the sudden death of a friend, and I found it effective in calming my anxious thoughts and flashbacks. It's recognized by the American Psychological Association (APA) and World Health Organization (WHO).

- **Cognitive Processing Therapy (CPT).** This is a structured type of cognitive behavioral therapy (CBT) that helps you identify and challenge distorted beliefs around your toxic-boss trauma, and is commonly used to treat post-traumatic stress disorder (PTSD).
- **Prolonged Exposure Therapy (PE).** Focuses on gradually confronting trauma-related memories, feelings, and situations. Helps you process the emotions associated with your toxic-boss trauma.

2. Somatic Therapies/Practitioners

There are many types of interventions that work on releasing emotions and tension from your body, which you can learn more about to determine if one may be a fit. These therapies integrate physical awareness and movement to release tension and the effects of trauma.

Examples include:

- **Somatic Experiencing (SE).** Addresses the physical sensations of trauma stored in your body. Focuses on regulating your nervous system and releasing trauma through bodily awareness.
- **Dialectical Behavior Therapy (DBT).** Focuses on regulating your emotions, increasing your distress tolerance, and mindfulness.

- **Emotional Freedom Technique (EFT).** A therapeutic approach also referred to as "tapping" that combines elements of cognitive behavioral therapy (CBT) with acupressure techniques. It can address your emotional distress and reduce stress by tapping on specific points on the body while focusing on an emotional issue or memory, like your toxic boss.
- **Neurofeedback Therapy.** Uses real-time brainwave monitoring to help you learn to regulate the activity in your brain to increase relaxation, focus, and emotion regulation.

3. Talk Therapy

Talk therapy helps you to explore your thoughts, feelings, and experiences to develop insights, coping strategies, and work toward healing from the toxic boss. Some modalities include:

- **Cognitive Behavioral Therapy (CBT).** Helps identify and challenge beliefs that have been distorted by the toxic-boss experiences (e.g., self-doubt). Focuses on developing healthier thought patterns and ways of coping.
- **Acceptance and Commitment Therapy (ACT).** Encourages accepting thoughts and feelings, rather than avoiding them, and committing to actions that are aligned with your values to change your behavioral reactions. Also integrates mindfulness.
- **Solution-Focused Brief Therapy (SFBT).** Focuses on building solutions to move forward, post–toxic boss. Includes goal-setting and rebuilding motivation in your career and life.

Crisis Support Lines

If at any time during your journey you feel hopeless and/or are having thoughts about ending your life, it's critical that you reach out for immediate support. I've included crisis lines in both the United States and Canada here, but if you are from other parts of the world, search for "crisis lines" or "suicide lines" on the internet to find support in your area ASAP. You *can* feel better and there *is* help out there for you. The world needs you in it, and please know that you *don't* have to suffer silently.

United States:

- Crisis Text Line: Text HOME to 741741
- Disaster Distress Helpline: 1-800-985-5990
- National Suicide and Crisis Lifeline: 988
- National Suicide and Crisis Lifeline (options for deaf and hard of hearing): For TTY Users—use your preferred relay service, or dial 711 then 988

Canada:

- National Suicide and Crisis Lifeline: 988
- For First Nations, Inuit, and Métis Peoples—Hope for Wellness Help Line: 1-855-242-3310
- Anxiety Canada: 1-800-668-6868
- Mental health resources for men specifically: https://headsupguys.org

Toxic Boss Articles

If you are curious to read other perspectives on toxic bosses, here are some articles from a variety of sources on the topic:

- *7 Bad Bosses to Avoid—and How to Spot Them During an Interview:* www.fastcompany.com/91165348/7-bad-bosses-to-avoid-and-how-to-spot-them-during-an-interview
- *Learn from the Five Worst Traits of a Toxic Boss:* www.forbes.com/sites/dedehenley/2024/06/23/learn-from-the-five-worst-traits-of-a-toxic-boss
- *How to Survive a Toxic Boss, Step-by-Step:* www.fastcompany.com/91132222/how-to-survive-a-toxic-boss-step-by-step
- *5 Ways to Cope with a Toxic Boss (Without Quitting Your Job):* www.forbes.com/sites/carolinecastrillon/2024/02/04/5-ways-to-cope-with-a-toxic-boss-without-quitting-your-job
- *How to Tell If Your Boss Is a Corporate Psychopath:* www.telegraph.co.uk/business/2023/10/23/how-tell-boss-corporate-psychopath
- *Bosses Should Fix Toxic Workplaces, Surgeon General Says. Here's How.:* www.washingtonpost.com/wellness/2022/10/22/toxic-workplaces-stress-surgeon-general
- *Why Every Leader Needs to Worry About Toxic Culture:* https://sloanreview.mit.edu/article/why-every-leader-needs-to-worry-about-toxic-culture
- *How to Recover from a Toxic Job:* https://hbr.org/2022/10/how-to-recover-from-a-toxic-job

NOTES

Part 1 Introduction

1. Green, James E. "Toxic Leadership in Educational Organizations." *Education Leadership Review* 15, no. 1 (2014): 18–33.
2. Schmidt, Andrew A. "Development and Validation of the Toxic Leadership Scale." (MSc diss., University of Maryland, 2008), 1–131, ProQuest (1453699).
3. Howington, Jessica. "Flexjobs Report: Toxic Managers and Coworkers Pervasive in the Workplace." *FlexJobs*, September 22, 2024. https://www.flexjobs.com/blog/post/toxic-managers-coworkers-make-toxic-workplace.
4. Brouwers, Marissa, Paltu, Amelda. "Toxic Leadership: Effects on Job Satisfaction, Commitment, Turnover Intention and Organisational Culture Within the South African Manufacturing Industry." *SA Journal of Human Resource Management* 18, no. 1 (2020): 1–11. https://doi.org/10.4102/sajhrm.v18i0.1338.
5. Sull, Donald, Sull, Charles, Zweig, Ben. "Toxic Culture Is Driving the Great Resignation." *MIT Sloan Management Review*, January 11, 2022. https://sloanreview.mit.edu/article/toxic-culture-is-driving-the-great-resignation.
6. Alterman, Toni, Tsai, Rebecca, Ju, Jun, Kelly, Kevin M.. "Trust in the Work Environment and Cardiovascular

Disease Risk: Findings from the Gallup-Sharecare Well-Being Index." *International Journal of Environmental Research and Public Health* 16, no. 2 (2019): 230. https://doi.org/10.3390/ijerph16020230.

7. Zadow, Amy J., Dollard, Maureen F., Dormann, Christian, Landsbergis, Paul. "Predicting New Major Depression Symptoms from Long Working Hours, Psychosocial Safety Climate and Work Engagement: A Population-Based Cohort Study." *BMJ Open* 11, no. 6 (2021): e044133–e044133. https://doi.org/10.1136/bmjopen-2020-044133.
8. Office of the Surgeon General. "Workplace Mental Health & Well-Being." *U.S. Department of Health and Human Services*, January 24, 2025. https://www.hhs.gov/surgeon-general/reports-and-publications/workplace-well-being/index.html.
9. Washington, Ella F., Birch, Alison H., Roberts, Laura M. "When and How to Respond to Microaggressions." *Harvard Business Review*, July 3, 2020. https://hbr.org/2020/07/when-and-how-to-respond-to-microaggressions.

Chapter 2

1. *Diagnostic and Statistical Manual of Mental Disorders: DSM-5-TR*. Fifth edition, text revision. Washington, DC: American Psychiatric Association Publishing, 2022.

Chapter 4

1. Mitchell, Kathleen E., Levin, Al S., Krumboltz, John D. "Planned Happenstance: Constructing Unexpected Career Opportunities." *Journal of Counseling & Development* 77, no. 2 (1999): 115–124. https://doi.org/10.1002/j.1556-6676.1999.tb02431.x.

Chapter 6

1. *Diagnostic and Statistical Manual of Mental Disorders: DSM-5-TR*. Fifth edition, text revision. Washington, DC: American Psychiatric Association Publishing, 2022.
2. Fincham, Guy W., Mavor, Ken, Dritschel, Barbara. "Effects of Mindfulness Meditation Duration and Type on Well-Being: An Online Dose-Ranging Randomized Controlled Trial." *Mindfulness* 14, no. 5 (2023): 1171–82. https://doi.org/10.1007/s12671-023-02119-2.
3. Ratey, John J., and Eric Hagerman. *Spark: The Revolutionary New Science of Exercise and the Brain*. Little, Brown Spark, 2008.
4. Noetel, Michael, Sanders, Taren, Gallardo-Gómez, Daniel, Taylor, Paul, del Pozo Cruz, Borja, van den Hoek, Daniel, Smith, Jordan J. et al. "Effect of Exercise for Depression: Systematic Review and Network Meta-Analysis of Randomised Controlled Trials." *BMJ (Online)* 384 (2024). https://doi.org/10.1136/bmj-2023-075847.
5. Workplace Bullying Institute. "2021 WBI U.S. Workplace Bullying Survey: The Complete Report." 2021. https://workplacebullying.org/wp content/uploads/2023/06/2021-Full-Report.pdf.

Chapter 7

1. American Psychological Association. "APA Poll Reveals Toxic Workplaces, Other Significant Workplace Mental Health Challenges." *American Psychological Association*, July 13, 2023. https://www.apa.org/news/press/releases/2023/07/work-mental-health-challenges.
2. Brassey, Jacqueline, Coe, Erica, Dewhurst, Martin, Enomoto, Kana, Giarola, Renata, Herbig, Brad, Jeffery, Barbara. "Addressing Employee Burnout: Are You Solving the Right

Problem?" *McKinsey Health Institute,* May 27, 2022. https://www.mckinsey.com/mhi/our-insights/addressing-employee-burnout-are-you-solving-the-right-problem.

3. Pittampalli, Al. "When Should You Trust Your Gut? Here's What the Science Says." *Psychology Today*, November 16, 2017. https://www.psychologytoday.com/us/blog/are-you-persuadable/201711/when-should-you-trust-your-gut-heres-what-the-science-says.
4. *Psychology Today*, "Intuition." https://www.psychology-today.com/us/basics/intuition.
5. Pogosyan, Marianna. "Understanding Interoception, the Sixth Sense." *Psychology Today*, August 24, 2022. https://www.psychologytoday.com/us/blog/between-cultures/202208/understanding-interoception-the-sixth-sense.
6. De Becker, Gavin. *The Gift of Fear: Survival Signals That Protect Us from Violence.* Back Bay Books, 2021.
7. Hutson, Matthew. "8 Truths About Intuition." *Psychology Today*, December 4, 2023. https://www.psychologytoday.com/us/articles/201912/8-truths-about-intuition.
8. Howington, Jessica. "Flexjobs Report: Toxic Managers and Coworkers Pervasive in the Workplace." *FlexJobs*, September 22, 2024. https://www.flexjobs.com/blog/post/toxic-managers-coworkers-make-toxic-workplace.

ACKNOWLEDGMENTS

I would like to express deep appreciation for my book coach and content editor, Suzy Vadori, who believed in this book from our very first lunch discussing the idea in 2023. Fitting book writing into my already busy entrepreneurial and personal life seemed almost impossible, but with Suzy's guidance, deadlines, accountability, and encouragement, I was able to get the book done in just over one year. Suzy helped me make this book practical and engaging, guiding me to find my authentic voice throughout.

Next, I'd like to express my deep appreciation for my publisher, Brooke Warner, from She Writes Press, who believed this book needed to be birthed at this particular time, and has been a joy to work with. Likewise, Shannon Green, managing editor at She Writes, has been extraordinarily organized and helpful in moving it along through the many stages of completion. I'm also grateful to the amazing copyeditor, Krissa Lagos, who contributed to the flow and succinctness of my writing throughout this book.

I would like to express how much gratitude I have for Renee Pi, Lea Kalinovska, and Shachi Saini, the university students who worked on various toxic leadership research projects with me from 2024 to 2025. Mentoring and learning from my talented undergraduate students has been one of the great joys of my career. Seeing you grow in your careers is a gift, and I'm honored to be a mentor along your career journeys.

A huge thank-you also goes out to the beta readers who took the time to give me valuable feedback: Téo Blackburn, Judith Sparkes, Dr. Kelly Tremblay, Jamie Vadori, and my supportive husband, Scott Lovett. Thank you to members of my team at Canada Career Counselling who gave feedback on therapeutic modalities and job search strategies, including Nina Hornjatkevyc, Ariel Hennig Wood, and Allison Lockett. Thank you also to Kira Del Casale, Kaylie Fulwiler, Fatima Debek, and Diana Bernier, all of whom have helped me as executive assistants and believed in the power of this book. Also, to Jennifer Huber, who believed I had an impactful book in me and the ability to bring it to reality.

Finally, thank you to my children, Nick, Matt, and Cadence, and my husband, Scott, all of whom have supported and loved me through the turbulent times in my career and life. I am so grateful for you; your support has made all the difference in this challenging but beautiful world.

ABOUT THE AUTHOR

Dr. Laura Hambley Lovett is an organizational psychologist, keynote speaker, business leader, author, and podcast host. She is a sought-after thought leader on workplace psychology and career development internationally, with twenty-five years of experience. She is a thought leader on the future of work with a deep understanding of the intersection of business and people.

Dr. Laura's areas of expertise include leadership, team, and culture development in organizations, remote/hybrid workplace success, toxic leadership, career development, and mental health/burnout. She holds a PhD in industrial/organizational psychology from the University of Calgary, where she is currently an adjunct professor.

A passionate entrepreneur, Dr. Laura has founded several psychology practices in Canada since 2009, including Canada Career Counselling, Synthesis Psychology, and Work EvOHlution™, which was acquired in 2021. She runs the widely followed podcast *Where Work Meets Life*™, which began in 2020, and speaks with global experts on a variety of topics around career fulfillment and thriving humans and organizations.

In addition to her businesses, Dr. Laura has published two psychological thrillers, *Losing Cadence* and *Finding Sophie*. Through these stories, she hopes to both captivate readers and raise awareness on important topics around mental health and domestic violence. Both books are currently being adapted for a television series.

Dr. Laura cofounded the WITH HER (www.withher.ca) movement focused on ending violence against women and girls in 2019. She also is chair of the board for a performing arts organization, the Youth Singers of Calgary, which was founded in 1985. She received a Canadian Women of Inspiration Award as a Global Influencer in 2018.